# VULVACIOUS

*Embracing Female Sexuality
and Sexual Freedom*

MICHAL COHEN SIMHA

Producer & International Distributor
eBookPro Publishing
www.ebook-pro.com

VULVACIOUS: EMBRACING FEMALE SEXUALITY AND SEXUAL FREEDOM
Michal Cohen Simha

Translation: Gabrielle Weiniger

Contact: vulvaciousonline@gmail.com

ISBN 9798393847005

*In loving memory of my mother, Amy Beth Cohen.*

*This book is dedicated to healing the female dynasty and to the creation of an existence built on respect, trust, and harmony between the masculine and the feminine.*

# TABLE OF CONTENTS

# VULVACIOUS

To liberate the vagina,
To free the vulva,
To relax into yourself,
Liberate sexually,
Free yourself,
Liberation,
Vulva,
Vagina,
Vulvacious.
To free the vagina
What?!
To empower the vulva,
You get it?
To release it!
To release what?
The vulva!!
Why?
What is there to be released?
A lot...
What?
A lot
Oh...
A lot
A lot of what?
A lot of liberation and freedom for the vulva
Oh...
What does it mean to liberate the vulva?
How do you even relax it?

I'm not even prepared to say the word,
Vagina
I said Vagina!
Ahh...
Vulva
I said vulva!
Breathe,
Dialogue with the vulva,
Massage the area,
Smile,
Even just saying the words,
"Free the vulva, free the vagina," frees it!
Cheers to the awakening to life
with a liberated vulva, a liberated vagina!
To sexual freedom,
To awakening!

# DISCLAIMER

This book is written primarily for a female audience, but can also be an excellent resource for men. Although it is written in the context of male and female relations, it goes far beyond the boundaries of gender. It examines both feminine and masculine forces, and it is therefore inclusive of — and relevant to — whomever may choose to experience an act of love with a woman or with another man. Forces of the masculine and feminine exist beyond gender but also beyond physical bodies. This book was written with the full intention of loving and respecting all people, whomever they may be.

# HOW TO APPROACH THIS BOOK

This isn't a regular book. From its very outset, it is written with the intention of you embarking on an investigative inner journey; a deep-dive into the depths of your soul, your sexuality, your power, and the way in which you choose to walk on this Earth. Everyone goes at their own pace and has their own way of making changes. Therefore, you may want to read the book all in one go or even choose to open the book randomly and read a chapter by itself. Each chapter will invite you to create an intention. Intentions generate their own power to create and manifest. Therefore, the mere act of choosing an intention in the form of a statement uttered out loud in the present tense will support you in building the reality you have asked for. To those looking to go a step further in their journey, write your intention down on a piece of paper including the action you want to take and the support you would like from the universe in order to see your intention realized.

*I wish you a blessed, gentle and honor-filled journey of inner growth and profound learning that will penetrate to the roots of your soul and connect you to the sexual woman that you are, across dimensions and new worlds that you have yet to encounter.*

# IT'S A SENSITIVE SUBJECT

Sexuality is such a delicate matter. We live in a society where the majority of people have been sexually harassed in some way or another:

A disrespectful glance, an unwelcome touch, unauthorized penetration, and extreme coercion.

Even our genitals have come to be used as swear words in many languages.

Men, women, boys, girls, elderly men and women have all been harassed over the course of their lives. A lot of tension has been created by so much pain, sickness, frustration, and the inability of people to communicate comfortably about sexuality and their sexual desires. It's both a visible tension and the kind of tension that penetrates the very air we breathe; it is unspoken and has generated so much hardship among so many people.

A lack of science and information on the subject of sexuality in regard to healthcare and self-nourishment has presented a challenge as well.

Our pornographic culture and the objectification of women and ourselves as women only add to the pot.

All of these issues lead me to write this book and pass on what I know: the knowledge of love, loving sexuality, the sacred union, and the ability to grow and evolve to empower ourselves through this sexual energy.

Sexuality is sensitive. Every person will have their own personal story about sexuality that is woven into their lives.

This book invites you to be open to a new way of thinking; to leave behind deeply-ingrained personal and societal preconceptions of sexuality and to have the courage to pave your own way and cross through any fear, jealousy, and guilt, to reconnect to passion and a life filled with pleasure.

The process can be simple and straightforward, but can also be complex, painful, and scary. I know with absolute certainty that meaningful dedication to relaxing and empowering the vulva, alongside a much-needed relaxation of attitudes around the subject of sexuality, brings inner peace and, ultimately, world peace.

*From the depths of my loving heart, I pray that more and more women are awakened to their own unique sexual power, and agree to empower and relax their vulva! May all women live a sexual life full of pleasure, love, desire, harmony, and peace. I pray that more men will choose to be men of love and will agree to bring out, through their sexual organs, the light of love, patience, integrity and compassion for women of love.
This is how we birth a world where the masculine and feminine is balanced, unified, and more complete!*

*Thank you.*

# INTRODUCTION

I awoke early, snuggled inside my comforter while observing the raindrops pattering on my window. A joyful smile brimming with anticipation rose upon my face. Part of me wanted to stay warm and cozy in bed, but an inner force roused me. Waves of excitement washed over me and filled me with happiness for the weekend ahead. I sat up in bed and sent prayers and threads of light and courage to all the women who were on their way, this very minute, to the workshop — to me. I prayed that the universe will support them and help them arrive safely. I got up from bed to wash my face, as I do every morning, and looked in the mirror, registering that knowing twinkle in my eye that is just for me, and with a smile said to myself: I love you. I bless this workshop with success. I agree to be a tool for knowledge that seeks to pass through me and arrive at this exact workshop today. Good morning sweetheart, I whispered to myself as I washed my face with lukewarm water.

All the other members of the house had left, gone away for the weekend. The workshop was set to happen in the yurt that acted as our living room. Raindrops always hit the yurt with great intensity. I was wearing my favorite outfit: a warm tank top, a vest with a soft, cozy cream sweater, and black leggings that have a colorful dragonfly print. According to Native American tradition, dragonflies symbolize the shedding of illusions.

I entered the yurt which is a wide, open circle and womb-like; so, very suited to this workshop. I burned a sage stick and orbited the space, purifying all negative thoughts, doubts, and fears. I thought about the women and the courage it took to come here and join the workshop, and I began to organize the center of the room to represent and reflect my deep intentions. I laid down a red velvet cloth and on top of it, a large rose quartz crystal symbolizing the love and sensuality that is at the heart of these teachings, as I so long for more women to learn to love every single part of themselves. I then placed a bouquet of white roses and white lilies in a jar beside the crystal. Flowers are the plant's genitalia, although they don't feel ashamed of their sexuality. Many of the flowers even look like vulvas. I wish, I mumbled to myself, that more women would look at their vulvas and relish the sight of them like they would a beautiful flower.

I placed a candle to mark each of the four directions of the wind, and next to each of them, an iridescent crystal to signify and invoke the four directional cosmic gazes. I took a deep breath and fed oxygen to the bubble of excitement that had nestled in my stomach as I prepared for myself some sweet, warm herbal tea. One last look — and yes, the space is ready. So am I.

Each workshop or ceremony of "empowered vulva" is different, both for me and the participants. New knowledge appears to me and I always discover that it is relevant both to me and to the women present. The degrees of embarrassment, worry, fear, and openness vary from time to time, but all these characteristics are always floating in the ether and come up sooner or later, together with a thirst to study something new about life from a place of deep recognition into the natural feminine mystery.

The rain kept falling. I looked out the window and I imagined the water washing the ground, cleaning and clearing the space anew. In another ten minutes the women would arrive, I thought to myself, just as a woman with curly hair and big, curious eyes entered the space.

"Hi! I'm the first one here?" she asked, slightly disappointed.

"Yes, welcome," I replied. "Help yourself to a cup of tea to warm you up. In a moment, everyone else will get here," I reassured her.

"I'm Ember, and I came in from Pardes Hannah," said the

woman, as she proceeded to sit down with a cup of tea in hand. "Tell me, where did you get the name for this workshop from? Seriously, it really got to me..."

I smiled. That was the kind of reaction that made me feel at home. "It's a long story that I'll share during the workshop. But, in short, a little bird sat on my shoulder and whispered: You're going do to this, and this is what it will be called."

It began to pour even harder outside. A few minutes passed and I began to be concerned. I wondered whether the participants had gotten cold feet and would not come. As soon as the worry landed in my heart, she arrived: A woman who looked to be in her 30s — tall, straight brown hair, with striking and sharp facial features, who couldn't be missed. I relaxed, feeling my sense of security return. I breathed deeply into the anticipation bubbling inside me. She smiled at me in greeting, put down her bag, and sat down comfortably, getting out her phone and quickly becoming engrossed in the screen.

Suddenly, a tall, heavy-set, and slightly older woman entered the yurt like a hurricane: "What is it with all this rain? As soon as I left Ra'anana I almost turned around and went back home, but I signed up for this workshop half a year ago and I've been waiting for it. I came but I am freezing. Where can I put my bag?"

"Here, take this and warm up," said Ember, handing the woman a cup of tea. "Put your bag here," she said to the woman as she gestured to an area close to the door where her bags were already piled up. "What's your name?"

"Beth," replied the woman.

"Come, sit next to me," Ember offered.

The door opened and more women entered the room. I welcomed them all. I was happy that, this time, women of all ages had joined the workshop. This will be interesting, I thought to myself. A woman in her 50's entered the space silently. She turned to a young woman and asked her gently, with a dash of apprehension, if she could sit next to her.

"Yes, of course," replied the young girl, "I'm Ellie."

"Nice to meet you. Ruth."

"Ruth is a name I haven't come across in a long time," Ellie said with a smile.

"In my sect, it's a common name," said Ruth.

"Are you religious?"

"Yes, I am from Jerusalem," Ruth answered. "And you?"

"I'm from Tel Aviv," Ellie said. "Incredible that we managed to get here from so far away even with all this rain."

I invited the women to sit in a circle. They sat down slowly. I asked them to put aside whatever went on that morning and to bring themselves here, to this present moment. The door opened again and an average-height woman entered the yurt, hunched over. I noticed sadness in her eyes. She apologized for her lateness and joined the circle.

The prevailing silence returned as the rain came down in the background and flames from the lit fire in the wood-burning oven crackled in the fireplace. I felt that the fire was talking to me, as if to remind me of both my life force and the natural, inner fire that burned within me and had sparked so very many life events that had unfolded and led me here. With that inner recollection, I began:

"Everyone, stand up for a moment and let go of everything that happened this morning at home and on the drive here by shaking your hands," I said, as I demonstrated the movement.

"We're always doing so much. Let go of the loads you are carrying, and the tensions that build up, please drum on your chest and make the sound 'ah'..." For some of the women, it was hard to make a sound. I asked them to pair up in twos and tap each other on the back in order to release the sound.

"When we release our voices," I said to the women as they tested their voice power, "we put aside all our thoughts about ourselves and our voice, whether we're faking it or not. Allow that sound, which is unique to each one of you, to simply come out. Projecting our voices will release our fears, worries, and anxieties, so let's do it! Let's let go!" My words of encouragement loosened their restraint and the women dared to make the sounds with ease.

I felt that we had arrived at the stage where we needed to sigh out loud, and I invited the women to sigh with me. "There's nothing like a good sigh to take off a load, allow us to be in the here and now, and stop those noisy thoughts that want to run endlessly through our minds," I sighed and continued: "It's just like making love: when the moans come out spontaneously, the body knows what to do and helps us to release the intense energy that flows through us during the sexual union, which quiets our thoughts and helps us to simply be in the moment."

The women were more relaxed this time and let themselves give out a freeing sigh more easily, comfortably, and even loudly.

"Come, let's sit," I asked after a little time had passed.

"Good morning!" I said with a smile, "Before we dive into our journey together, I want first and foremost to agree amongst us all that everything personal that is said in this room will remain between us. You may all share your own personal journey to whomever you please, but don't share other women's stories that you hear here, ok?" I cast a glance at each woman, making sure that every one of them confirmed what I had asked with a look or a nodding of the head.

"So, let's start by clarifying why we're here. We're all gathered at this 'empowered vulva' workshop to deal with the subject of sexuality. It's important for me to emphasize that this workshop is done fully clothed. There are workshops in the field of sexuality that are done naked, but this is not one of them!" I said smiling. "We've come here for a two-day workshop. When we break for lunch, I'll show you to your rooms; they're right here in the house, close by. Rose will cook us our food for dinner tonight and all our meals from then on. As for now," I said, "I would love it if everyone could say a few words about themselves, and why they came to this workshop."

"My name is Iris," began one of the women. I was surprised; I didn't expect her to be the first one to talk. "I live in a *village* in the Sharon plain, and I was really nervous about coming here, but I decided that I have to make a change in my sex life," she said decisively.

"Have to, or want to?" I asked.

"Want," Iris replied with a shy smile.

"The word sex is fairly broad. What do you really want?" I asked her.

She smiled, embarrassed, but took a deep breath and said: "That I will even want to have sex in my life in the first place."

"You're here, at this workshop to empower and relax your vulva. It's a sign that you have already chosen, and want sex to be in your life," I said, "so what do you want from your sexuality?"

"I want to feel desire," Iris said quietly, "for desire to simply be a part of me to help me want to have sex."

"Thank you," I said, and turned to the woman next to her: "You're welcome to introduce yourself and share why you are here."

"I'm Ember; I live in Pardes Hannah. I'm 31 years old, and not in a steady relationship. I've already participated in a lot of workshops connected to sexuality," she said and continued without taking a breath: "What do I want and why did I come? I don't really know. I do know that the title "empowered vulva" intrigued me, and I really want a relationship. maybe if I empower my vulva, it will help..." she said, half laughing, half giggling bashfully.

"Thank you," I said to her and turned my gaze to the person next to her.

"My name is Ruth. I'm a mother of four and a senior doctor at Hadassah Ein Kerem Medical Center," said the woman as tears rolled down her cheeks. "My husband and I separated a year ago and I'm having a hard time. I miss him; he hurt me, and I don't seem to be able to let him go. I feel as though he's squatting inside my body."

The tears cleansed her face. I looked at her lovingly, knowing within myself just how much healing her tears are bringing to her heart.

"Would you like to share with us what you are looking to get out of this workshop?" I asked, "Try to turn your focus inwards and figure out what you are looking for today, from this retreat."

Silence filled the room. Ruth took a breath — this time fuller and deeper — and said: "I want more peace and quiet in my life."

"Thank you, Ruth," I said. "That together with your tears succeeded in identifying a deep-seated need. With inner peace and quiet we truly are able to cope with anything, even when we are facing challenges."

"I'm Ellie," a young girl who was part girl, part woman continued the round. "I'm 20 years old. I think that I'm probably the youngest woman here. My friend recommended this workshop to me and I came to learn more about life."

"Thanks, Ellie," I turned to look at the woman next to her.

"I'm Beth, the grandmother of the gang. I'm sure I could be most of your mothers, and it really embarrasses me to talk so openly. But I must do this for myself. Over the years, thick layers of discomfort have accumulated around sexuality. That's why I'm here."

"Beth," I said, and looked deep into her eyes, "what do you want?"

"To take off this load and be lighter and more straight-forward with this topic. That's what I want," said Beth.

I continued to look around and my eyes came to rest on a woman, around 30 years old, with long, straight brown hair and big, kind eyes. My gaze fell on her with a smile.

"I'm Carol," she said, and with her hands made a stop sign as if to tell me and the circle that that was all she could manage to say right now. I respected her wishes with a loving look and continued on to the last girl who had not yet introduced herself.

"I'm Noa," she said quietly, "I really didn't want you to get to me... I want to learn more and to accept all aspects of myself," she

19

continued in a voice so quiet it was almost impossible to hear, but bravely carried on, "I want to learn to accept my sexuality. Most of the time it doesn't come easily to me, and even saying this now out loud in front of a group of women, it's really outside my comfort zone. So, that's it, thanks for listening," she finished in a quiet, slightly trembling voice.

My heart filled with gratitude on hearing that she had found the inner strength to tune in to the deepest desires of her soul, in spite of her fear and anxiety. I took a deep breath, the kind of breath that helps me center myself to clear my thoughts and retrieve the information that would bring forth what I was going to say next:

"Well, I think we're about done introducing ourselves," I acknowledged with a smile, when suddenly the sound of rolling thunder echoed outside. Everyone turned towards the window. "Wow... It seems there's a lot more waiting to be discovered in the day and a half that we have together. The skies are trembling and opening for the blessed rain to fall and cleanse us."

I breathed deeply into the numerous different expectations and intentions that we had all placed in the center of the circle and I invited the women to take a deep breath:

"Alongside the cleansing rain that came with us to the workshop, so too are sunrays of pure and bright light that penetrate down from the sky. I'm guessing you've all noticed that I use the word 'intention' a lot. Intention is like a clear, illuminating ray of light," I said. "A clear sun beam of choice that expresses our will and the conditions or the thing that we seek to manifest in our lives. It could be to strengthen a feeling or emotion, or something substantial and tangible such as creating a loving partnership, earn more money, build a home, or travel abroad. It can be big things or small things. But it's important that the intention, just like a ray of light, will be well-defined and pronounced clearly, so that the universe, which supports us in every moment to create our realities, will fully understand you. When the universe understands, it sends you support. If you are clear, you will know which action to undertake in order to make your desired reality be realized, but also, of course, you must dedicate yourself to the unknown.

I paused for a moment and observed the group of women who were listening to me with great concentration. When a full smile had filled my heart and become visible on my face, I continued: "With great joy I am setting a clear intention that this workshop will help grant each women present personal feminine empowerment."

"I'm assuming that your intentions are: to broaden loving and respectful communication with the feminine sexual being that you are, to deepen your relationship with your yonis[1] from a new and transformed space, to recognize your feminine-female qualities that embody you, and to learn to be in peace with masculine energy. I request help from the Creator in clearing out old patterns of thinking and behavior, beliefs, and relationships that are no longer aligned with this new reality for myself and for every one of those present in this room. Thank you, thank you, thank you!" I stopped for a moment and allowed the intention to be present in the space.

"Come, let us breathe in that intent together," I invited the participants to join me. "Check if you agree with it, check in with your inner self that the intention I have placed here matches your true will, and that you wish to devote yourselves to it."

"The female empowerment part I understand, and the connection to the vagina, great — let's go for it, I'm in," said Ruth, "But what do you mean by 'in peace with the masculine energy.'"

"That refers to the deep knowing that the creative power of life is masculine and feminine, eggs and sperm, circle and line,"

1. The word 'yoni' comes from the Sanskrit word for vagina. It refers to the female sexual organs or a symbol of them, especially as an object of veneration within certain types of Hinduism, Buddhism, and other cultures.

I replied. "Everyone who agrees to work with these forces and cooperate with them in our everyday lives will have the spirit to create and bring their gifts to the world more easily and more powerfully. Is there anyone else who doesn't connect with this, or something else in the intention?" I asked, turning my attention to the other women.

"What does 'deepening my relationship with my vagina' mean?" asked Ellie.

"An important question," I said, "part of the reason that you came here today is to awaken your vaginas to a new level of awareness."

"Sorry," interrupted Ruth, "I find it hard to believe that I even said that word out loud in front of a group of people. What exactly does awareness there mean?! The vagina feels?! Knows something? Ultimately, it's just another body part. Yes, through it we birth children, but what are you referring to?"

"There are studies that prove that the body responds to the way we treat it," I said quietly, "Water, for example, responds to words. Our bodies are made up of 70% water, and therefore respond to the way that we treat them with words in thoughts, feelings, and actions. If we tell the vagina it is ugly, it will feel ugly, if we say that it is pretty, it will feel prettier. We can speak to our body parts and to develop a more beneficial relationship. I am inviting us to create a more beneficial relationship with our vaginas."

"How did you get involved in this field of the vulva and sexuality," asked Iris.

"This is a good opportunity to tell my story," I said. "A few years ago, I got a message that I have a huge gift to give to the world on the subject of sexuality. I had no idea what I was supposed to do with that message and what gift I had to give to the world. I was a yoga teacher and I conducted personal sessions and group meetings to balance the human electromagnetic field, but in regard to sexuality, when it came to dwelling within it or even talking about it, I had no idea or prior experience. I dove into a brave and, at the same time, rather terrifying journey, researching subjects like sexuality, womanhood, manhood, femininity, masculinity, victimization, empowerment and choice. But even at this very moment, as I'm sitting in front of you and talking, it's still a process that is both emboldening and freeing me from very deep personal and collective patterns associated with womanhood-sexuality-femininity. The ability to choose to agree with, study from, and to listen to my vagina, is an art form. Much of the time I simply don't understand; either that or I am really afraid of what I am about to understand. I had to gather a lot of courage to embark on this journey, and it takes more and more courage every minute to overcome my shyness and simply talk about sexuality."

A fallen log thudded into the burning fireplace. Ember got up and added more firewood to the flames. For years, I've been aware of the universe speaking to me and giving me signs all the time. While everyone's attention was pulled into the fire, I had a moment of quiet observation where I was able to breathe and muster the courage to continue speaking about myself and the awakening of my sexual energy. Ember returned to her seat and I kept talking.

"Thanks Ember, for feeding the fire with more wood. So, at the age of 41, I realized that I had lived most of my life in secret, hiding away from being a sexual being. I hid it from others but especially from myself. I identified deep feelings of shame, and noticed a fear of the very great life force that flows through me. As I researched more and peeled away the outer layers, I started to feel, sense, and understand that the vagina feels and senses the world around it. The more that I work within this frequency, the more I live a fuller, more powerful, happier life.

I took a deep breath, into the base of my spine, and continued: "When the vagina clenches, it stops feeling and sensing the world that is flowing into it, produces a thick armor like a terrific chastity belt that acts to both protect and choke us alike. Sound familiar?"

I asked — and continued without waiting for an answer. "I know that the world that we live in was and still is truly dangerous to walk around in with a freed, empowered, and awakened vulva. But I want to help you get to know a new way of thinking; a way that says - if we dare to connect and to be in touch, we will claim back our power. We will go into the meaning of that particular sentence later on, but for now suffice it to say that each one of us will be safer in the world. We will be able to free our vulvas and live a life of fulfillment with all the wondrous variety of layers that come with it. All this can happen through the use of abundant energy sources that are naturally available to every woman.

There is a movement of sexual energy in the world, both on a level we are conscious of and on a level that we are not aware of. Many a blocked heart seek to open to others' love and sexual love. The world is also filled with a deep fear of life: fear of the sexual energy pulsating through us as well as a lack of knowledge of how to guide it and give it a place. The world is full of shame, constraints, misrepresentations, and suppression. And, at the end of the day, what does a person want? Life, movement, beauty, fulfillment, love, and prosperity," I said with pained yet radiant eyes.

To live a life that feels like life — alive and full of vitality — we are required to be brave and have courage to move beyond who we perceive ourselves to be and towards self-love in its many aspects. Sexuality is a part of those very aspects that make up the whole being that we are. I've spoken a lot," I said, "Come, let us once again take a deep breath; it's a knowledge that it is worthwhile to breathe in, to allow it to sink in and be absorbed into our body's cells."

"Wait, wait," Ember jumped in. "How is self-love connected to the empowered vulva... I don't understand this at all..."

"Self-love is the key to a life with boundless inner peace," I turned with a look of love to every one of the women present. "There will be more peace and quiet within us when we occupy

24

ourselves with being kind and not self-critical. When you, and you, and you, love yourselves, your vaginas, and the sexuality that is part of you, your lives will be easier, more straight-forward, and more harmonious. Now, it's time to be in silence," I said. "Please close your eyes and relax your forehead, your eyes, and your jaws. Allow your entire face to be limp and free of tension. Place your palms over your vaginal area and breathe into your lower abdomen and your womb; and from there, into your vagina. Inhale into the vagina and exhale out of the vagina to the rhythm of your natural breath. Feel what happens when you breathe into your vagina. Maybe you have never breathed into it before, or maybe only during childbirth — all of those are ok. Maybe the air, or the life force reaches there, and maybe it doesn't. Any and every feeling that comes up is welcome. Now, I invite you to say to yourselves in your heart: I am a sexual being. Say it again in a whisper, so that it's almost inaudible to the person next to you: again: I am a sexual being. And again: I am a sexual being, in a whisper out loud. "

They said aloud: "I am a sexual being," and again, louder: "I am a sexual being."

"Be with that, play with the statement in your heart, as an incantation, in your regular voice and out loud."

All the women in the room whispered the statement in a quiet voice and then out loud. The room filled with laughter and slowly, but surely, a feeling was formed that this statement was indeed legitimate, that it was safe to declare that we are sexual women.

"Great," I said, "now close your eyes and take a deep breath, bring your attention inwards and notice how you feel now. Please say in one word a feeling that comes up for you."

Words came up in that room that describe the feelings of every woman in the world: "Happiness," "shame," "embarrassment," "funny," "passion," "creativity," "love," "pain," "fear," and "power."

"Thank you," I said. "Now is a good time to pluck up more courage for an in-depth investigation into the mystery of the feminine[2]. I invite you to discover more from your special, unique inner spring, from the well of life that we hold.

"When we study and deepen our connection with the vagina and our understanding of the life force that dwells inside us, we become an abundant spring. Let us agree to derive pleasure from it, to give and to receive more."

The women opened their eyes again and every single one already looked different, like the spring water had already started to wash over them and to bestow upon them its gifts. Outside, it continued to rain unabated, as though it came to cleanse the earth of old patterns and allow new seeds to awaken and sprout afresh.

After a few minutes of silence, I felt a wave of emotion and curiosity come up within me for the women in front of me. I was happy with the atmosphere of security and openness that we had begun to create, both in the physical space and within myself.

I prayed that this openness would only grow, that everyone, from their own private places, would dare to come out and meet with more chambers within themselves, that they had not yet encountered and maybe didn't even know existed.

"I'm cold," said Iris, "May I prepare myself a cup of tea?"

"Wait," I said. "I want us to look into each other's faces, into each other's eyes. See if something has changed." The women gazed across the circle as drops of rain fell in the background, as though playing a tune on the window.

"Yes, I swear, there is something...cleaner in almost everyone's faces," said Beth in wonder.

"I see it, too!" said Iris.

"Good. So, make yourselves a cup of hot tea and return to the circle," I said. Almost everyone got up and prepared themselves tea. Carol stood quietly opposite the fireplace and looked into the

---

2. In Hebrew, the word feminine, 'nekevah,' comes from the root-stem letters n, k, and v, that is to say, orifice or hole in the earth where there was a lush spring of gushing water.

fire. I looked at her and her strong presence and I hoped internally that she would find a way to express herself as the workshop went on. I prayed to myself that she would have the courage to bring herself to the fore in this workshop and in life in general. The smell of chamomile tea mixed with the smell of coffee. A few minutes passed and most of the women had already sat back down in the circle, a cup of warm tea in hand.

"Come, Carol, join us," I invited her and she came back and sat down. Ellie sat last. "Great," I said. "We mentioned our sexuality and honed our ability to say it out loud, at least in this forum, so — wow - I am sexual. How wonderful! So, let's continue."

*With an energy of love and joy, I choose to expand communication of love and respect with the sexual being that I am, I deepen the relationship with my yoni from a new and deferential state of mind. I ask to be supported by the universe to clear thoughts, patterns, behaviors, outdated beliefs, and relationships that no longer serve me, so that I may create a new reality for myself. Thank you, thank you, thank you!*

# WHAT IS AN EMPOWERED VULVA?

"Even saying the word vulva out loud used to be hard," I said. "The wee-wee, down there, fanny—all kinds of nicknames, literally every name in the book—except the word vulva. Amidst all this shame and embarrassment, I said the word vulva for the first time in public when I was 29 years old. I was hosting a ceremony at a woman's retreat and, a moment before the ceremony, a tantra teacher whispered to me to tell everyone to liberate, empower, and relax their vulvas. I had no idea about the field of sexuality, it sounded strange to me, but this was coming from a respectable and well-known tantra teacher, so I did what she said. I took a leap of faith and I said the sentence, with no inkling of just how very far I was from understanding the profound essence of those words or the journey I had just embarked upon by agreeing to empower and relax my own vulva.

"The yoni is the most private, intimate, and sacred space for every woman. A gateway to life and creation, a gateway to pleasure and desire that nowadays is cloaked in so many layers of shame, suppression, and endless patterns of fear.

"Each one of us sitting in this room was created and given life from the meeting of sperm and an egg, and, usually, between a penis and a vagina. It's the foundational moment of existence for each and every one of us, so how absurd is it that so many people have such enormous difficulty in even saying the word vulva comfortably out loud, with due respect and recognition to the sacred energy and life force that the vagina grants to every child, woman, and man born on Earth."

I stopped to listen to my surroundings. The yurt was so quiet and through the window, I could see rays of sunlight dancing on the raindrops that were balanced atop the leaves of the oak tree, twinkling magically, a tender union of light and water.

"When I say, 'empowered vulva,' what do I mean? What do all of you think?" I asked, "I want to hear what everyone pictures when I say that, what goes through your minds?"

Ellie ventured to start: "To empower the vulva sounds to me like being free to go to bed with whomever I want," she said.

Iris continued: "Maybe it's the chance that, finally, I will actually want to sleep with my partner and that I would even feel like doing it in the first place."

"Let's start from the fact that I can barely even say the word vulva," said Ruth, "so maybe to empower the vulva means to be willing to say the word or to talk about my vulva comfortably," she giggled sheepishly and continued: "Look, I've already said vulva three times in one sentence—so I have empowered and freed my vulva!"

The women laughed together and, suddenly, the atmosphere felt lighter and more relaxed. The laughter stripped off one of the layers of embarrassment and created a freer space for Beth to speak her words next:

"Look at me, I could be a grandmother to some of you. I'll share my issue with you. When I have sex, my vagina is dry. I've put on all kinds of ointments and oils and still, it gets dry so quickly. I think it's mostly an issue for older women. So for me, freeing and empowering the vulva means going back to being wetter, to a vagina that has more moisture, that's less dry and tough."

"Thank you for sharing so openly and honestly," I said with excitement, delighted at the safe space we had created amongst ourselves. More women shared and, at the closing, Ember spoke up:

"Honestly, all of you have said such fascinating things here, but if I am being honest with myself, I have no idea what you mean by empowering the vulva. I'm really intrigued, but I just don't understand what you're getting at, Michal." She said this with a big smile, her curly hair flying in every direction. But underneath the smile and relaxed facade, I could see a look of concern. Her brows were furrowed and she appeared to be under a cloud of frustration.

"Nonetheless," I insisted, "take a breath for a moment, turn your attention inwards. When you hear me say, 'empower your vulva,' where does that touch you? Where do you feel it in your body?" Ember released a heavy, liberating sigh.

"Good," I continued. "Breathe deeply into your vaginal opening and ask your vagina what she needs to release." And as a spring flowing in harmony and in constant movement with the Earth, the words flowed easily and simply from Ember's vagina as she said: "To develop the ability to be more serene, with less dramatic and angry, emotional encounters with men. To be a calm, relaxed space when encountering the male domain. And to be less stressed out from interacting with men."

"Thank you for sharing," I said. In the background, logs crackled in the flames from the hearth. I ventured on to say: "Like the flames of the fire that are always changing, in color, size, and sound, I invite each and every one of you in this workshop to investigate what an empowered vulva means to them. We are all different and so everyone will have their own unique experiences and their own answers. Sometimes, your answer might even change from moment to moment. I invite you all to the process of profound perceptual change. Change in how we walk through life, how we show up, and how we fulfill ourselves as women of this world with female sexual organs. With a warm, healthy internally burning flame.

"In Sanskrit, the ancient language in which sacred Indian-Hindu writings are scripted, the word for vulva is yoni, meaning the source of all life. It is a sacred space that refers collectively to the womb, the ovaries and fallopian the vagina, and the cosmic vulva of generations of women that both were and will be born into this world. I invite us to remember our deepest recollections, born from generations and generations of women who have

31

walked on this planet, with the origin of all life within us, standing with this in the world in the presence of peace. The vagina is a gate, an entrance to the life energy that flows through us, in all kinds of situations, not only in times of making or acts of love. Our vulva has an opening just like a mouth, she is open and energy flows through it, going inside and out. When we consent to move around in this world with this knowingness, our vulvas are given respite and healing."

An air of excitement filled the room, laced with curiosity and wonder. Some of the women were looking at me with a quizzical look as if to say: "How on Earth do we do that, what are you going on about?!" Others seemed more comfortable and relaxed, experiencing the joy of starting to relate to the language of their bodies at long last. I took a deep breath, the kind that always helps me center myself and brush aside any fears or anxieties. I felt the energy build up in preparation for the deep, intimate process that the discourse on sexuality would bring into this space.

"Good, let's take a deep breath," I said. "Place a hand on your vaginal area and breathe into it."

"Wait," said Ember, "What do you mean, breathe into the vagina? How is it possible to breathe into an organ in our body? We breathe into the lungs, not to the..." Ember hesitated a moment... "Vagina... wow, how very hard it is for me to say that word."

"Vagina, vagina, vagina.... Ember, I'll answer you on that shortly," I said and continued: "I know that we aren't generally used to putting a hand on our vaginal area in public, so a moment before we do that, in order to release any discomfort in the body, and from any shirking away from saying the word vagina...," I smiled with a twinkle in my eye, unleashing the playful and lighthearted girl that I am: "Let's say the word vagina all together, out loud, in a whisper, laughingly, let's do it—ready, set, go!"

"Vagina, vagiiiiiiiiiinnnnnnnaaaaaa, vagina." The women said 'vagina' in all kinds of variations and tones, carefree and full of glee, filling the space with the sound of the word.

"Amazing! We are so awesome! Now, I invite you to close your eyes," I said as the commotion began to subside a little.

"Collect yourselves and turn your focus back inside. Yes, good! Bring your attention to your face and let it hang loose. Once again, place your hand over your vaginal area and breathe into it. If you're not able to breathe to your vagina, breathe into your lower abdomen, as close to the vaginal area as you are able." I waited a moment and let them try out the experience of breathing into their vaginas. For some of the women, it would be their first time experiencing such sensations, but I knew that others wouldn't manage to sense anything.

"Great. Wherever you get to with your breath is just fine, be with whatever comes up. The breath is one of the main gates to the energetic flow of life to the body.[3] When I breathe and direct my breath to a certain area of the body, the consciousness that is the life force will reach there. If you pay extra special attention, some of you might even feel movement within the labia's, a sensation that it is expanding and releasing. Take an inhalation into the vagina and release an exhale from the vagina, from your vaginal opening. Feel your vaginas, be with them in full presence and in awareness. We will stay here with this together, with the breath, everyone at their own pace, for a few more minutes."

They all devoted themselves to deep breathing into the vagina. The room was quiet enough to hear the sound of the air entering the body and the air leaving the body.

"Even if you don't feel your vagina, that's fine. Try to breathe in the direction of the hand that is placed on the vaginal area and pay attention to the movement that reaches your hand. If the movement doesn't reach your hand, that's ok too.

Everyone has their own body and degree of sensitivity—and skill when it comes to breathe awareness to body parts. The more

---

3. In Hebrew, within the word 'breath,' 'neshima,' lies the word 'soul,' 'neshama.' It can be interpreted that the breath allows more of the soul to enter the body.

you practice, the more accessible this technique will become for you." The women continued deep-breathing, their faces were slack and relaxed, and I felt a stillness envelop me. The initial excitement from the start of the workshop had begun to dissipate. I breathed in unison with the women.

"Now," I said, "I'm going to ask you all to alternately squeeze those ring-like muscles that are found inside your vagina and anus and to release. Great!"

I waited to let them practice sensing their vaginas through the movement of the circular muscles of the pelvis.

"Let's move to the next stage, which is a little more challenging. I want you to play with squeezing the anus muscles by themselves, separately from the circular muscles in the vagina. It might be really easy for you to separate them, but for others it may be more difficult. Whatever you manage to do is just fine and correct. There's no right or wrong here. Just find a rhythm for moving the ring-like muscles inside your vaginas."

I waited a few moments and continued: "Maybe you'll feel sexual arousal, meaning that this exercise is actually a pleasurable experience. I welcome you to just allow yourselves to be with any sexual energy that comes up. If you're not feeling sexual energy that's also fine. Every feeling that comes up in the body is welcome. Continue to breathe through the opening of the vagina, the lower abdomen, the womb, or whichever section of your lower body you manage to get to. Now, I want you to address your vulvas and ask them: what does it mean to be empowered?"

Ellie started to shift her body in discomfort. Her breath became shorter and she was moving from side to side. I gazed upon her lovingly, a respectful supporter of the hard feelings that were coming up for her.

"I'm sorry for interrupting the meditation or the breathing that you are doing," she said, "but I really don't understand. You want me to speak to my vagina?!" Ellie settled down, her eyes watchful. I smiled at her pleasantly.

"I'm suggesting that you try," I said. "This whole workshop is a bit out of the bounds of our normal day-to-day reality. Just start to talk to it, ask it. I practice doing that a lot. Just chatting with my body, asking my body parts what they want or need from me, how they feel. Perhaps there are some people who may think I'm hallucinating, but I really believe in what I'm telling you. This is a practice I've been following for many years now, ever since I was a yoga teacher. I believe that attentive, in-depth conversations with our bodies, or with a part of our body individually, supports our mental and physical wellbeing—and gives us the most reliable answers."

Ellie closed her eyes. I saw that, although she didn't completely understand what I wanted her to do, she completely devoted herself to the practice, returning to the rhythm of deep breathing in the direction of her vagina. I saw that she did indeed succeed in bringing her awareness to her lower stomach. A good sign.

The room remained quiet. After a few minutes had passed, I placed a piece of paper and a pencil in the hands of everyone in the group and explained what I wanted them to do.

"Earlier today, I asked this question and you gave an answer from your minds. Now, I want your vagina's answer. What does it mean to release and empower the vulva, as per your vulva? The moment the answer comes to you, write it down."

To my surprise, Beth, the elder of this amazing group of women, was the first to take the pencil and start to write, quickly followed by Ember. Each one of the women opened their eyes and began to scribble. I was happy to see that Ellie was writing.

"Great! I see that everyone has finished," I said. "I invite you all to share briefly what it means for each one of you to free and empower the vulva, according to the inner dialogue that has come from direct communication with your vaginas."

"I'll start," said Ruth. "I am an ophthalmologist at a hospital. The idea of speaking to a body part, after studying medicine and having over 50 years of life experience, is strange to me. But then again, even to come here in the first place is not my usual way. So, I've chosen to go even more outside of my comfort zone. I inhaled into my vagina, as you asked. At the beginning, it was hard for me, but seriously, very slowly, I actually began to feel the passage to my vagina. I felt that something was landing there, something was happening, thanks to the way I was breathing with awareness, directing my breath somewhere specific in my body. So the answer that I got from my vagina was to relax, release, and calm not just my vagina, but my entire body."

"Thank you, Ruth," I said, and Ellie, the youngest of the group, took over: "As I said before, it was weird for me to speak to my vagina. I am only 20. I've only just been released from the army[4] and I've never heard of speaking to my vulva before. It's totally new to me. I think that I have never got in touch with her in a personal way and actually, I felt that she was really glad that I had finally got in touch with her and talked to her directly." Ellie began to laugh and the entire room filled with an undulating female laughter. "It's funny, but seriously, I felt that my vagina was happy that I spoke to her, so a released vagina for her—basically, for me—means that I connect with it, to its signals and requests. That's the answer that I got, but to be honest...," said Ellie, "I don't fully understand that answer."

"And you want to understand it?" I asked.

"Of course, that's what I came here to do: to relax and empower the vagina," Ellie answered mischievously.

"Thank you, Ellie," I said. "We will talk more about how to relate to the vagina's signals and requests, or how the vagina even signals, speaks, and indicates to us, a little later. Who wants to go next?"

"I am 45 years old, with three children," Iris began. "All three births were difficult: traumatic, painful, and unpleasant. The

---

4. Author's note: In Israel, both boys and girls are obligated to join the army at the age of 18.

answer I got from my vagina was that she is asking to be breathed into. I realized that throughout those births and actually, in life in general, I haven't really breathed. I do not breathe, I'm constantly contracting and clenching my entire body. So it's not only breathing into my vagina, it's the awareness to pause to breathe, to relax at all."

"Thank you, Iris," I said. "Are you all noticing how our discussions are broadening in scope? The conversation isn't just around the vagina. It is shining a light on the bigger picture, on our way of life in general. To relax and empower the vulva means making a deep-seated change in our entire life perception, through the prism of sexuality. This change needs us to approach it from a new angle, with all the worlds and layers that make us who we are, so that we can set aside our thought patterns and the way of life we were taught growing up. We will learn to use the totality of the whole life forces that we are composed of, without ignoring or repressing the vagina and the feelings that come through it. The vulva is part of the wholeness that we are."

Beth joined in: "Now I'm in my golden years and I got the answer that my vagina glows when she's relaxed. I asked her, or me—that separation between myself and my vagina is still a bit weird to me—what is a glowing vagina? And I got an answer that surprised me. To be at peace with my body. As you all can see, I am full-figured. After years of dieting, going up and down in weight and hating my body... My vagina is asking me to love my larger body. That is almost impossible for me. I hate my massive stomach, and anyway, what has it got to do with my vagina?! I don't remember the last time I put a hand on my vagina and touched it. Another answer that my vagina gave me was that a freed vagina is a wet vagina, full of fluids. Like I shared with you all earlier, I suffer from dryness down there. I have a lot of work to do in order to attain a free vagina.... Right now, I feel like I have to get up and leave here, it's too much for me." To everyone's surprise, Beth abruptly stood up, took her bag and moved to leave the room.

"Beth," I said, "if you want and feel that leaving is really the right thing to do for you, that to walk out now is part of your journey and growth, I respect your decision. I understand the difficulty in staying. The material that comes up here is not easy for anyone. I have no way to even begin to describe the way through some of the fears I had to experience in order to bring this workshop to light and to come out with the book soon as well. It's a very scary path that demands much courage from the women who walk it; to leave hard-trodden patterns and agree to come face-to-face with parts of ourselves that perhaps we didn't even know were part of who we are. I want to offer you another way. We want to stand up for you and be here for you in this difficult moment that has arisen."

A silence fell in the room. No one knew what Beth would choose to do. Deep down, I had a strong feeling that she would choose to stay, but I clearly saw the parts that wanted to escape and not deal with the pain. Ember, who had already formed a small bond of affection and love with Beth earlier in the morning, stood across from her. Ember, who had already attended a few workshops on the subject of sexuality, awareness, and development, stretched out her arms and let Beth choose whether or not to receive a hug. Beth complied. She approached Ember and looked at her wordlessly, giving her consent. Beth sank into Ember's embrace. One by one, the women stood around them, encircling them. Some women placed a warm and loving hand on Beth, others told her that they loved her. Noa reached for the guitar that lay in the music corner and began to play to her and sing quietly, a song of angels. Every so often, I chimed the crystal singing bowls, their sound reaching to the very depths of the soul, every cell in the body vibrating with its intensity.

The room was transformed into an endless sanctuary, filled with a special atmosphere of acceptance and love. Beth began to cry and even Iris, who, until that moment, had stood awkwardly on the side, softened, putting her hands on her heart and beginning to cry, too. It was a moving moment that had erupted spontaneously among a sorority of women, sisters to the journey, who had known each other a mere two hours and yet already felt their comradeship on their shared path. A path that called on the women of the "tribe"— created an hour ago—to unite, for the benefit of one of them who was experiencing unexpected difficulty.

Beth, too, succeeded in standing up for herself. Indeed, when a woman is attentive to herself and listens to her inner voice, who does what she really wants to do, the entire universe will support her passage.

"Everyone, take a deep breath," I requested. "Be aware of your heart, your vagina, your throat, your head, and the soles of your feet. Breathe into the body wherever it is asking for your attention. Beth, how do you feel?"

"I am at a loss for words," Beth said with tears in her eyes, "I'm touched. I've never felt so much love all in one go, and from women that I don't even know! Thank you. I am staying. I know that you'll be here for me the next two days and this calms me."

I looked at the women and said: "I want to say thank you to each and every one of you for what just happened here now. I'm moved by the speed in which this happened. How much love and kindness you have brought to Beth and to every one of you who is present in this room. A magnificent sisterhood is one of the ways the vulva can be liberated relaxed and empowered. When there are women surrounding you who love and respect you and when you are able to share both the hardships and joys of life with them. I give huge thanks to what happened here. It means a lot more to actually demonstrate the value of sisterhood than to simply talk about it. May you all create more and more space for sisterhoods in your daily lives. It's one of the most genuine tools to truly permit the vulva to be freed and empowered."

All the women got up and went to sit back down in the circle. Ember stood, made a cup of tea, and brought it to Beth, who was already seated. The room had a pure feeling of close intimacy and love. I was very happy about that. I knew the journey the women were going through together was going to be deep and meaningful for each one of them; that was something I knew inside myself no matter what. Still, before every workshop, I always had to cross wide expanses of fear; fear over who would come, whether the contents I would bring will suit them, how they will receive the teachings, and various other anxieties.

"What sweethearts we all are.... How many times have we criticized ourselves," I said, "and made remarks about ourselves? This is the moment to say what a nice person I am, what a sweetheart I am. Put the palms of your hands on your faces and say: I am so good and cute."

The room filled up with embarrassment and silence once again. "Come on, say a kind word to yourselves, please," I implored. I placed my hands on my face and said out loud, "I am cute and sweet." Slowly but surely, the rest of the women told themselves that they, too, are good and sweet.

The declaration raised the energy and created a light, pleasant atmosphere.

"Great. How do you all feel now? Don't you agree that it feels good to say kind words full of goodness and love to ourselves?" I asked. "We are living in a society that teaches us to be very critical towards ourselves and towards the world. I truly encourage you all to implement these loving thoughts and say kind words to yourselves as part of your day-to-day practice in your everyday lives. Now, we can move on," I said and looked around the women's circle.

"Is there anyone else who wants to say what their vulvas told them about what it means to be empowered and relaxed?"

Ember nodded and her voluminous, curly hair moved with her head. A necklace with a white, shining stone glistened on her neck. "An empowered vulva listens to the rhythm of her body. My necklace is called a moonstone. From certain angles, you can see the colors of the rainbow and it reminds me of my lunar cycle."

"Your lunar cycle?! What is that!" Ruth asked in a tone somewhere between contempt and ridicule, part disparaging, part doubtful.

"That's my monthly cycle," said Ember, "the tide that moves inside me between my blood time coincides with the new moon, sometimes called a 'black moon,' and the time of ovulation, that can correlate with the full moon. Between those times, there is the continual cycle that takes place inside of me. Time for becoming full, in preparation for ovulation, and time for depletion that leads up to the blood time. The word *menses* doesn't in fact refer to the time of menstruation, but rather indicates the cyclical nature; the flow, the cadence, which takes place in our bodies."

"Thank you, Ember," I said, "that's important knowledge for each one of us. Part of the work to empower and relax our vulva is indeed understanding our inner rhythm. Ruth, did Ember's answer satisfy you?"

"Yes, but I don't fully grasp how it helps me to understand my rhythm, because my periods are all but over for me," said Ruth, "I didn't chart my cycle. I would even go so far as to say that every time my period arrived, I would be pretty bummed out about it. If it wasn't for the fact that it enabled me to have children, I could have easily given it up."

"It's important that you're bringing this up here," I said. "We will discuss the topic of menstruation and the significance of the cycle during this workshop, and thank you, Ember, for sharing your knowledge. I encourage all of you to share anything that you feel is relevant to our workshop.

"Everything that you have brought here reflects different aspects that encompass the essence of a released and empowered vulva. But I want to highlight a few things at this point. At the level of the physical body, a released and empowered vagina refers to a vagina built from a strong, functioning pelvic floor, who knows how to clench her muscles and let them go. It's not a weak, sagging vagina, with muscles that are too loose. It is a living, breathing vagina, one that gradually releases the energetic and physical contractions within the vaginal walls and from the inner and outer lips. The vagina is a gate and through it, energy flows in and out. Part of what goes into us enters without us even noticing; and sometimes, when we do pay attention, it makes us clench ourselves from inside. The whole area around the pelvis; the hip joints, the lower stomach, the womb, the anus, the perineum—that's the area between the opening of the vagina and the anus—is directly related to the vitality of our vaginas. Our mouths and jaws are also connected to our vaginas in a direct fashion, because the circular muscles of our mouth, vagina and anus work together. And, of course, our awareness, thoughts, and emotions affect the state of our vaginas. We are an entire system and it is impossible to make a separation between parts. Everything is connected to everything else. From that place of wholeness, we are going to talk about the vulva and how to deepen our understanding and our recognition of the importance of treating her respectfully, lovingly, and attentively. How to treat the vagina to ensure less muscle contraction in both the physical and energetic body."

"Energetic body?! What is that?" Ruth's question interrupted.

"An important question, thank you, Ruth," I replied calmly. "We have a physical body that is built from all kinds of parts, but in essence, we are a lot more energy than material. The base, the primary spark for the creation of life first happens in our energetic body. The energetic body, like our physical body, is built from all kinds of structures and parts. In Chinese medicine, for example, acupuncture is done through meridians, an energetic system that sits within the physical body. Part of the contractions that we have in the vagina are physical and we see them—as we see a muscle contract, but part is energetic—in our energetic bodies."

"And what comes first? The contraction in the energetic body or in the physical body?" Ellie asked.

"The energetic body is the first to respond, because it is directly connected to our emotional and intuitive body," I said. "You know that feeling when something is about to happen? That's the energetic body; the physical body is responding to the energetic one. Am I being clear? It's really crucial that you get what I'm talking about!" I said as I looked around at all the women to be sure they understood me. I saw their faces were still and composed, eagerly drinking in the information that was coming through me, and I felt happiness in my heart.

"Do you have other questions or ideas about the concept of the empowered vulva?" I asked.

"I'm trying to understand," said Ellie, "if part of relaxing and empowering the vulva means that I should be passive when I'm having sex?"

"No, it means that you shouldn't be tightening it," I answered. "When you are passive, motionless, it's supposedly easier to let go. But that's not always the case. There are situations where one can be passive and yet, the entire body is clenched and frozen. Relaxing the vagina refers to letting go from the inside, an inner freedom in body and soul. And that, if and when difficult emotional or physical issues arise, they are not ignored and shoved aside, but dealt with, not carrying on as though nothing happened. That is the art of letting go while in motion, responding in the moment from a space of internal attentiveness. Relaxation here means consenting to expansion, to tenderness, to love, and to contain the loving energy that flows to you. Does that answer your question?"

"Yes, it more than answers it," answered Ellie in quiet equanimity.

"Are there any more questions?" I looked around with interest.

"Yes," said Iris. "What do I do when I experience reluctance or a contraction in my body or in my vagina during sexual relations?"

"Breathe, that's the first thing that's always worthwhile to do," I answered. "You've asked an important question and we will expand, deepen, and elaborate on it as the workshop goes on, including what to do in a situation like that. In the meantime, let's take a lunch break. You're all welcome to take out the treats you brought from home and eat them together in the kitchen. It is in the room next door. I also want to show you to your rooms where you'll be sleeping. You can go and put your things there now."

The rain kept falling. The women got up from their places and got out their food. Some of the women stayed lounging on the mattresses and others went to the bathroom. A few of them began to chit chat amongst themselves while the rest remained contained inside themselves, seemingly digesting the new information and energy that had passed through the space. In the kitchen, the table was now filled with wonderful delicacies in a wide variety of colors. The women were hungry and they devoured their food with liveliness and passion. When they had finished eating, I left with them to the house next door and showed everyone to their rooms where they would be sleeping. Meanwhile, I went back to my bedroom to rest.

Towards the end of the break, there was a respite from the rain. When I returned to the yurt, I saw that Ember and Beth had gone outside to smoke cigarettes. Beth was hugging Ember again. I was happy to see the special bond that had formed between the two of them, a bond that had crossed the age gap and their different lifestyles.

*I choose to learn what a freed and empowered vulva means to me.*

# HOW DID WE GET HERE?

I sat down in my place and started to play the crystal and Tibetan singing bowls. With the new, pleasing sound of the music in the background, I invited the women to return to the circle. The chatting stopped. The sound of the bowls initiated a gentle transition from the regular to the sacred. The women dedicated themselves to the sound. Some sat upright, others leaned on cushions, and a few lay down on the mattresses, resting their hands on their hearts or on their faces and letting the music take them away. A feeling of fatigue hung in the air after a delicious, filling lunch. I let the women rest a little while I sounded the bowls and played in the background. The vibration from the bowls reverberated in the space as I began to play on the Native American drum I had built myself. The drum beat, which I love to refer to in a more feminine way as the 'drum beats', began to pound quietly and in full presence, like a heart, reminiscent of the primal heartbeat of life. The rhythm soothes every cell in the body, for, after all, the first constant rhythm that can be heard from the womb is the heartbeat of the mother.

I inhaled deeply and sensed the frequency currently present in the room. Every time I make this workshop, I am happy anew to see the women make the choice to grow, to dare to dismantle the patterns that they had grown into, ancestral patterns created by generations upon generations of women. That takes a lot of courage. It's a bravery I know well from my own experience. So very many times during my life I have been asked to dare, to go beyond the accepted norms. As I drummed, I realized a small ceremony was on its way. Although I hadn't planned a ritual for this part of the workshop, a big part of the art of guiding a retreat is to be attentive to the moment. What does this moment call for? To feel the call in all of your senses, to trust and to devote yourself to the moment. I know that when a ritual wants to come through me, it will come, it will manifest itself and create itself, and facilitate a transformation for everyone present.

I devoted myself to the drum beat, to the inimitable movement that was seeking to come through me at this present moment, and I started to talk: "Beloved women, so precious and brave. You came here today to empower and relax your vulva, to change a fundamental way of being in your lifestyles. You are invited to listen to the beat of the drum and offer yourselves to it, to move to the beat. You can do that sitting or lying down or standing up. Be authentic with your bodies."

All the while, I kept drumming the sound of a heartbeat. In time, the women started to move their bodies. I increased the pace of the drumming and its intensity. Beth got up and tentatively began to move her hips, softly and gently and in circles to the beat of the drum. With every movement the hesitancy from her body disappeared and more vivacity and beauty radiated from her.

"Great," I said encouragingly. "Connect to the rhythm of the drum, to the movement of your bodies, allow yourselves, yes! Great, how beautiful you all are! I invite you to close your eyes, to connect to the movement inside. Focus on the hips, move them, move the area of your sexual organs."

For some of the women, it was difficult at first, but it was evident that the movement was contagious. The space that held them allowed them the confidence to move and feel the freedom of the body, the hips, the pelvic and the vaginal area. Feminine beauty beamed out of them. How beautiful it was to see the women feel relaxed, move their hips and their pelvic area. I observed them and could identify, according to their freedom of movement, for whom it was easy and for whom this was harder;

who was able to move their hips freely and whose pelvic is frozen or immobile.

"I invite us to move deeper, into our relationships with our vulvas. Dance her, *be* the vulva, all of you, become one big vulva. Each one of you  is a vulva," I said as I continued to drum. The sound of laughter from ridicule reverberated through the room. I sensed that the laughter was derived from embarrassment and a difficulty to commit, so I continued: "Yes, I'm guessing that most of us have never danced our vaginas before, have never given all of ourselves to becoming one big vulva in any conscious way. It can be scary, but it can also be nice. Come, let's see what comes up. Consent to being present in the moment with the sensations that arise. You are invited to move around the room with the movement of the vulva. Breathe deep into the vagina and into the vaginal opening and let the vagina experience being all of your insides. One and all, dare to be one big vulva. Great!" I encouraged them.

The women moved around the space. Some of them widened their movements, becoming bigger and taking up space and others still caved inside themselves, as though frozen to the spot. Beth moved her body in heavy slowness. With time, more and more movement came into her body, increasingly intensifying and becoming stronger and stronger, and soon tears started to wash her eyes and the skin on her face began to glow. It was clear that she was going through something meaningful, essential, and healthy.

Ember was hopping and skipping from place to place, smiling, laughing, dancing in clockwise and counterclockwise circles, moving right and left, one moment jumping and the next, stopping to suddenly lie down on the floor, panting with excitement.

Ruth stood frozen to the spot, trying to move her body, but with great difficulty. Her face was pale; she looked as though she wanted to move her body so very much, but simply could not. Mental and physical lethargy eroded her and simply did not allow her to move. I continued beating on the drum. I gently moved closer to her and stood next to her. Looking at her lovingly and compassionately, I drummed, with the back part of the drum facing in the direction of her lower back. Initially, Ruth was resistant, but in spite of her fear, she gave into herself and allowed the beat of the drum to reverberate through her body. Her sluggishness gradually dissolved and she began to move.

Ellie, tall and upright, stood in one spot, practically immobile. She was mainly moving her head, her long hair spilling over her face and covering it. I went back to her and returned to guiding the breath in the direction of the vagina, connecting to the movement that flows from the opening. Ellie's movement started to change. Her hips began to gyrate in circles, her breath deepened and it seemed as though something had softened inside her. On the one hand, it was a challenging experience, yet on the other, freedom and power had entered into her dance.

While drumming, I began to sing a song derived from my womb, created by my inner strength. It was an intuitive song and the sound that emerged from me penetrated through everyone around me, deepening the process the women were going through. Another layer had been peeled off. More of the women deepened their breath into their vaginas, allowing a new flow to gush through their bodies, like electricity that had charged them with more voltage and power to illuminate their light in the world.

I was moved. When I guide a ceremony, I don't always know what is going to happen. I always have a feeling and a clear intention, but each moment has its own magic that is created out of grace from the wholeness of the moment and the women present there and their readiness for change. I felt that something had been opened. I slowed the rhythm of the drumming and I moved on to stroke the crystal singing bowl, creating a gentle but high-pitched sound, a sound that awakens the cells of the body and the DNA, calling on them to evolve. The women slowed the pace of their movement and one by one came to a stop. Ember lay on the mattress, relaxed; Beth sat on a pillow, leaning against the wall, her head tilted back; Ellie was sprawled on a mattress and a pillow, half lying, half sitting, peaceful, breathing deep breaths, her face loose, yet puckering at the same time, as though immersed in the process of dealing with a flood of thoughts.

"Take a deep and full breath," I said. "To the vaginal opening. Relax your faces, relax your jaws, and remove the tip of your tongues from the upper palate, close your eyes, and unfurl your forehead. Breathe a deep, restorative breath to the vagina. Listen to her and ask her how she feels, how you all feel being in a moment of awareness with her, when you are all vaginas."

"What pleasure," Ember purred aloud and burst into laughter, dragging more women into hysterics with her. Noa, who at the beginning had looked terrified, melted into the laughter that was echoing around the room. In my heart, I felt a deep gratitude for the medicine that laughter brings to the world.

The laughter subsided and the sound of everyone deep-breathing together remained.

"Let's all share in one word how you feel now and how you felt before," I instructed. "Don't move, do it while you are sprawled out in your places and relaxed."

"I am tired," stated Ellie.

"I was scared to death, I almost froze, but now, I feel better," said Ruth.

"Liberated," said Beth.

"Emotional," said Ember and after her, the other women volunteered spontaneously: "peaceful," "loved, "flowing," "sharp," "frozen," "tight," "amused," "pain," "really emotional," "powerful," "all-knowing," "dying from fear."

I gave internal thanks for the moment and I continued.

"Thank you, dears. Please rest your hands on your vaginal area and just say thank you, tell her that you love her. Pay attention to how that feels. Flood your yoni with love, imagining a pink light interwoven with gold that fills your yonis."

Tranquility reigned, with an atmosphere of sanctity and grace. Everyone's faces were soft, calm, and peaceful.

"Breathe deeply," I instructed, "into your vaginal opening and feel, sense, imagine or think about the lips of the vagina opening as air enters in. The opening of the vagina widens and when you empty out the air, feel the energy collected inside. Let this conscious movement be present inside yourself."

I decided to sing a song using the words of the first verse from the 'Amidah,' the standing prayer. "O Lord, open Thou my lips; and my mouth shall show forth thy praise." The melody filled the space in the room.

"You're all welcome to join me, even if you don't know the tune. Hum it with me, the words will come to you soon enough."

A few women hummed while others joined in singing. A profound, moving prayer song seeped inside our bodies and vibrated their very cells. An exhilarating ambience was formed from the union of all the sounds amalgamated, as the song permeated the veins of everybody present, at once soothing and causing them to tremble from within. The shared singing gently amassed an extraordinary, uplifting feeling. It was the feeling of an open heart in answer to a deep request from the soul, for everyone to open their lips—the lips of their mouth, the lips of their vulvas—the labia. After almost ten minutes of chanting, the volume lowered and there was quiet; the stillness of a group in great reverence, flooded with infinite love for all in the room.

The silence was broken by Ember: "Well, well... I've never experienced anything like that before. What a moving experience, such a special connection. We met only a few hours ago and yet, we are already sisters on a crazy, exciting, touching, heart-opening journey to liberate and empower our vulvas."

"Literally empowering and freeing our vulva," said Ruth, "I still can't believe how relaxed I am with saying that word now."

"Alright, beloveds," I said, "Let's go back to sitting down cross legged." I muttered a blessing and prayer of thanks for the wonderful supplication that came to us and for the support of the universe in this process until now.

"I am thankful to all of you for your dedication to this process, and give thanks to the support of all creation. I am aware of my prerogative to be a vessel for this exciting journey and for the wonderful support we receive so that this process unfolds in harmony, in grace, in love, in this room, in this place. Thank you," I said as I closed the palms of my hands together in namaste, the gesture used in India as a sign of gratitude and as a way of saying that we respect and recognize the divine of whomever is situated in front of us.

Out of loyalty to my own method and in recognition to the infinite ways and possibilities that one can navigate through the breadth one's own life, I asked: "How do you think we, as a society, have reached a state in which so very much has been obscured in regards to the vulva? A state in which most women in the world don't have a day-to-day connection with their yonis and wombs? A state where women don't possess an understanding or any knowledge at all as to how their vagina looks and of what she consists inside? A society that has a high rate of women giving birth by Caesarian section, where men have become the supervisors of departments of gynecology, where many women experience pain during penetration, dryness in the vaginal canal, a lack of sexual desire? And a society that doesn't recognize the power of a woman and the strength that she would be awarded if only for a daily connection with her yoni?"

"Truthfully," said Ellie, "in my entire life, I've never looked at my vagina."

"Do you reckon that in 65 years of life I have never looked at my vagina?" interrupted Beth. "Well, never in my life have I done that.... The idea never even crossed my mind— never. What would I even gain by looking at her? Even without looking, I know she is really gross. I know it's not nice of me to say, but she really repulses me, this yoni of mine, as Michal, you like to call her in Sanskrit. Honestly, I don't have an intimate relationship with her."

"Have any of you looked at your vaginas recently?" I asked.

"I have," said Ember, adding, "for a long time now, I've been attending a wide variety of workshops that are about sexuality and female empowerment, and that was one of the first tasks that I got, so I took a mirror and I looked at my yoni. At first it was weird. I looked at her and I really noticed that I went through this experience of rejecting my vagina, so I took it upon myself, as a mission, that once a week, I would take a peek and look at her. With time, I fell in love with her more and more. Today, when I look at her, I simply see a beautiful flower. I think it's really worthwhile for all of you to start looking at your yoni, to meet the flower that you all have. At least, for me, it did so much good. Since seeing my yoni as a flower, I feel much more beautiful and actually just generally better about myself."

"Thank you, Ember, for that important and sincere answer," I said. "I invite you all to get inspired, to free and empower your vulva and to look at her in the mirror. We live in a society where most women develop this attitude of 'live and let live in regards to their vaginas. We as women do not know exactly how she looks, we kind of reject her, regard her with disgust, and feel frustration when we receive our monthly flow. When we get a vaginal infection, then we smear ointment over her and then just shut her up until the next time. There is not a deep understanding about the specific parts that constitute the vulva, how she looks, or even how to touch her in a peaceful and comfortable way, using a diverse assortment of different pleasurable practices.

"A lack of familiarity with the vulva and experiencing that rejection removes us from ourselves, from our power, and from the complete and full acceptance of all of our body parts. The vulva will know what it is to be unloved, how it feels to experience a lack of affection and inattentiveness. That's one of the reasons why she is contracted. What do I mean by all this? You know that feeling the moment the lingam—that's the word for penis in Sanskrit—penetrates us, when it hurts you? Or, maybe, at the beginning, it feels really good and then suddenly the penis touches a place in the vagina where it simply hurts us?"

A few of the women nodded their heads. I carried on: "That's one of the examples of when a vagina will contract. If you place a finger in the vagina and press inside the canal every which way, you will feel places where it feels nice and other places where it really hurts. The vagina is much like a mouth, it's an opening for energy to flow. There is constant, shifting movement there and it will change inside on a day-to-day basis, depending on its energy collection—that includes physically inaccurate intrusions into her space that create a contraction that will then go up and accumulate inside her. If and when you are aware of any inner tension, there are various different ways to release it."

"What ways?" asked Iris.

"I will elaborate in due course," I said. "For now, let's talk about any other reasons why vaginas might contract. First thing we've come to understand is that the majority of women simply aren't truly acquainted with their vaginas. What else?"

"Sorry that I'm not about to answer your question," said Iris, "but for me, the experience of penetration is not exactly a great pleasure. I'm basically just waiting for it to end quickly. But at the same time, I am disappointed when it is over too quickly. I don't really enjoy the sexual act, but I really would like to experience real pleasure. In reality, when it happens, everything feels cold to me, fast and not pleasurable at all, and then I usually feel disappointed, hapless, discouraged from the whole situation and just generally helpless. I don't know what to do to change all that..."

"Thank you, Iris, for sharing," I acknowledged. "Part of your remark leads us to the next subject I wanted to talk about, regarding why we constrict our vaginas. The vagina feels offended, pitying herself and victimized—not really desired, and in the end, agrees that she doesn't want this, that the penetration came too quickly and she didn't say anything. She wasn't touched exactly how she wanted and she didn't speak up, just swallowing the unpleasantness. All these and countless more situations are examples of experiences of victimhood and to the victim-like vagina. Do you know these kinds of experiences?"

"As you were talking about it," said Ellie, "straight away, I thought about the feeling when a man penetrates me and then just finishes so very quickly that I haven't even had a chance to enjoy it at all. Straight away, I am disappointed, bummed out, feeling sorry for myself, but obviously, I don't dare say anything about it."

"You should know there are amazing man out there who really know how to hold in their ejaculation," responded Ember. "They are able to keep going for a long time. Intercourse doesn't have to be like you're describing it."

"This isn't nice for me to say," said Ruth, "I am a successful doctor and people come to me from across the country for treatment, but my sex life was exactly as Ellie describes: an experience of endless frustration, dissatisfaction, and ongoing misery. She is 20 years old and I am 50. Do I still have a chance to change that? How did I not realize while I was still young that something wasn't right? At least, now I am discovering there is another way. To wait to meet the right man, not another one of those men who enters you, finishes fast, turns his back on you and goes straight to sleep. I am not able to accept this inside my vagina, not even for another second. I don't believe that, finally, all this frustration has left me; I feel so very free. Something is happening to me here in this workshop. I feel more comfortable to talk!"

"Ruth dear," I said. "Chances are that your mother didn't know any different herself, that she wasn't taught this either, and so she didn't teach you. Most people have a huge gap in their knowledge. Even girlfriends barely talk among themselves about the small and intimate details relating to sexuality. So, what are we meant to do with vaginas that feel miserable? What are you doing when you feel neglected?" I asked, as a thick silence hung in the air.

Beth answered: "Have pity on myself, of course!"

"So, when we feel that we are unfortunate, how would we most want to treat ourselves?" I asked.

"Lovingly," Iris answered.

"Right," I confirmed. "So, before we dig deep into the issue of loving our vulva, let's try to understand more about what the experiences of wretchedness and victimhood are and how they affect us. Are you familiar with the general experience of feeling sorry for yourselves? With no particular connection to sexual encounters."

"Of course," answered Beth. "This entire horrible phase where my period ended, or the menses, as you say Michal, was simply a nightmare for me. The hormonal changes in my body finished me off. I wanted to die, I felt doomed, until one day, I said to myself: stop, enough with being a poor soul. At that same moment, something changed. Slowly, but surely, the situation improved and I found a way to balance myself hormonally."

"Thank you, Beth," I said. "That's a wonderful example of a situation where you transformed from a victim to a moment where you chose, in your strength, to take back the reins; you found balance."

"Isn't the word victim," asked Iris, "too harsh, too extreme?"

Suddenly, there was a loud clap of rolling thunder. The lights went out and then immediately came back on. "Whoa, I see the skies are also speaking to us and awakening us to this challenging subject," I said. "Right, yes, the word victim can raise difficult connotations." Another clap of thunder shook the room and the women instinctively moved a little closer to one another.

"Sorry that I am stopping here in the middle, but I really feel like drinking tea. Maybe we can go out for a short break?" Noa asked quietly.

Every time that I talk about victimhood, there is something external that tries to prevent me. I know the desire to stop. Challenging subjects really don't want to be discussed.

"Wait," I said. "True, it's raining and stormy outside, but we have a warm fireplace where we can add more logs, we can get closer to one another, too, and, in a little bit, we'll take a break," I said and continued to explain: "Victimhood mentality intersects with suffering and self-pity. Sometimes, it comes with the experience of power or a lack of it—that something is being taken away from us, a lack of control over a situation in our lives. It can even come with mental or physical pain and fear. Right now, I'm not referring to the severe examples of violence, rape, or physical injury. As I understand it, we live in a society where it is cool to live a life from a perspective of misfortune, because 'if I am unfortunate, then I deserve this' and that helps us achieve things we want. The concept of victimhood is very warped, as there are so many variations and it makes rather surprising appearances in our daily lives. Am I being clear? Are there any questions?" I opened the floor to the women.

My question was answered with silence, so I continued: "There are collective patterns of women that pass from woman to woman, from generation to generation by way of DNA, and this is a collective awareness that we carry within ourselves in layers that are not always apparent, information that is encoded into our collective vulvas."

"I'm sorry," said Noa in a soft voice, with an angelic, but also impenetrable look of curiosity. "I don't understand your question. What is a collective vulva?"

"Perhaps one of you might have an idea?" I asked the group members.

"Collective means something in common, something that belongs to everyone," said Ruth, "so if I take what you said, I understand that you are talking about the one big vulva, of all the

56

women in the world. In my life, I have never thought about that notion until now."

"Yes, that is exactly what I meant," I said supportively. "The universal vulva that bears the overall female memory inside her, that is connected to the womb and to our female genitalia. Memory that passes from generation to generation, from mother to daughter, and is expressed and looks similar for many women," I clarified a little more on the idea. "So, which memories sit there? What do you all think?" I refined my question.

"What ideas you have, I'm in total awe of them! Even in general, I'm in total awe here. Where on Earth do you get this stuff from?!" said Beth in amazement, with a hint of a smile.

"Men," stated Iris, before continuing: "Women, in their collective awareness, in their collective vagina, hold a deep fear of rape."

"Correct," I said, "and what else comes up for you all?"

"It doesn't have to be rape," said Ellie. "What about fear from a disrespectful look that causes us to feel bad?"

"Most women hold this collective consciousness of fear inside themselves, fear of becoming victims of wrongful penetration, without permission and consent, into their most private and sacred space, the vulva," I said.

"Sometimes the danger is real," said Ruth. "How do you separate between that and between patterns that are set off automatically?" she asked.

"That is a very good question," I said and added: "What do you do? How do you stop that endless chain of pain?"

"I have to say something," Ember interjected, continuing: "In some kind of way, we as women are inviting this reality to come into existence, by thinking that thought often enough, by many people. That thought holds power. As women, we invite this thought from fear, and yes, some of those incidents are real and I don't wish to belittle them, but we bring it on ourselves simply because we are so very afraid...."

"Are you mad?!" said Beth in disagreement and with rising anger. "These despicable men think they have ownership over us, they dare to rape us and you say that we women are to blame for that?"

I wanted to reply, but Ember was quicker than I.

"I am not saying the men are in the right. I am only saying that we, as women, should be able to take responsibility over our thoughts and to imagine something new. To stop fearing so much and imagine trust instead; and mainly, to give credit to the inner power that each woman has within themselves."

"What power? Do you even know what suffering sexual abuse brings? It's a whole life of torment and suffering," Beth retorted in defiance.

"Wait, let's stop this argument," I said before Ember had a chance to answer back. "Let's agree that you are saying two different things, but both are true and an existing reality. We can agree that abuse creates a magnitude of pain and suffering. And it has a really wide effect, as it has power far beyond what we can imagine, or even understand and perceive."

A barrage of rain hit the window, behind which a tremendous oak tree was billowing in the wind. The torrential rainfall startled the women in the room, embodying the tempestuous conversation of the universe with me and with the circle that sat around the room.

"The storm outside reflects the storm inside," I said. "I return to the question of how to stop the chain of intergenerational suffering that we pass on from mother to daughter. How to release the patterns that produce fears that are not always relevant and helpful to our current realities, fears that mainly just scare us and create avoidance. On one hand, the fear is here to protect us, but on the other, it blocks the sexual energy, our instinctive and creative vitality becomes stuck, obstructing our safe passage through the world."

My gaze fell on the window and on the gray clouds, where a ray of sunlight suddenly shone out spectacularly as they parted for a fleeting moment. I continued and cast a glance at Ruth. "When we are strengthened, all-embracing, and dare to do away with the fears pertaining to our vaginas, to undo the chastity belt that they put on us or, alternatively, that we put on ourselves, we will be able to be fully present, fulfilled, confident, and with an unsullied ability to communicate our desires. As long as we will be in a supportive sisterhood of women and in communication with our vulva, we will live with greater autonomy and in less suppression and shame. It will change the energetic balance between men and women and we will be in less danger."

"It will be like, a thousand reincarnations until we get there," said Ruth.

"Right," I said, "but every small step we take is meaningful and releases our daughters and also our men from these patterns, creating room for something new to come into being. We need to equip ourselves patiently and to take responsibility for the formation of inner change, as well as for the ways in which we educate our children. To change the way in which we speak about sexuality within our friendship circles and with ourselves. All this will create ripples of influence and change. We don't even know what the wave we make can do and how to measure the influence it will have on the world."

"I'm taking us back a bit, but you mentioned earlier the idea of a victim-like vulva. Are you ready to expand on what you meant?" Ember requested.

"What do you all say?" I opened the question for the women around me.

"It's a submissive vulva," said Iris.

"It's a vagina that experienced violence and non-consensual penetration inside her," said Ellie.

"Are you referring to rape?" asked Ember.

"That's an extreme instance," I answered for Ellie, "but it could also be that moment where we have an encounter with a partner and didn't really want to give our permission to enter but also didn't really say no. We didn't want to do it, but regardless, we cooperated. Have you encountered these kinds of situations?" I asked. The women nodded sadly.

"Obviously, I know that situation," said Iris. "Most of my life, I have found myself in sexual encounters that weren't exactly what I wanted and in most of those scenarios, I didn't manage to say no. I didn't even understand that I had the right to say no."

"That's an important point," I said. "Rape is rape and there is no argument that it is violent, forceful, and harmful. But there are sexual encounters that haven't received a clear obtainment of permission. Most men don't even think to ask the woman if he is allowed to enter into her yoni. In that case, it is obvious from the get go that he is not very respectful and that creates a contraction in the vagina and turns her, in most cases, into a victim-like and submissive vulva."

"Sometimes, I feel like my vagina is like a little girl," said Ellie, "insulted and feeling sorry for herself when a man that I like tells me no. I think that that is also a kind of victim-like vulva."

"For me, I simply can't stand it when the man inserts himself and then comes really fast inside of me," said Ember. "In that moment, I felt frustrated, like he betrayed me or deceived me and didn't see me at all, like I didn't exist. I experience this kind of emptiness. My vagina gets really disappointed from those kinds of situations. A victim-like, frustrated vulva that basically doesn't feel comfortable enough to say that she was disappointed from the experience," finished Ember.

"I call her the 'needing to please' vulva," I said. "A vagina that doesn't feel desire and doesn't say so because she's afraid that the man will leave or that she will get hurt, so yes, she, too, is a victim vulva."

"In my mind, a victim vulva," Beth started to say in an uneasy voice, "is a vulva that wasn't touched exactly as she would have wanted in that moment. I thought that I had good sexual relations with my husband, may he rest in peace, but now I'm realizing how many times he touched me there and I would cringe. I never told him. I let him lie with me and I just shirked away."

"When you say 'there,' are you referring to your vagina?" I asked carefully.

"Yes... Come on... 'There' is my vagina, our vagina," smiled Beth. "That word embarrasses me. All my life, I never said that word and now, aged 65, you want me to start saying vagina? There you go: vagina, vagina, vagina, vagina, to free the vagina...," she said and laughed heartily. The rest of the women joined her in laughter and all of them said the word vagina at the top of their lungs, then softly, fast, and then slowly again. I smiled.

"Beth, after all that laughter and fantastic release we just experienced here, I want to come back to what you shared," I said. "First, are there any other women here who can relate to her experience? Just raise your hand if that's something you've experienced," I asked. I felt a hint of shame and anxiety as the hands rose. I raised my hand and almost all the women raised theirs after me.

"So, you see, Beth," I said, "your story is not only yours. It's the same story for many other women. It's a painful story, one that makes us flinch, and at the end of the day, not only taints relationships between couples, but also distances the woman from herself, the man from himself, and from the women to whom he wants to make love. The men aren't always aware of what a woman is going through.

Quite often, it's especially during love-making that we lack the basic connection needed for openness and sharing.

"Of course," fumed Ember. "Who, exactly, taught me to communicate using words during love-making? Who taught me what to do during love-making? Or explained even a little of the technicalities of the process? In my opinion, there is barely a mother in the world who conveys that information or teaches these things to her daughters," Ember finished, sounding indignant.

"It can make one quite annoyed," I said and added: "This knowledge has been forgotten and stopped being passed through the generations. That's why the changes we are going through here are so very important. We are taking responsibility and educating our girls and the boys differently. We are unraveling the genetic chain of a victim-like and resigned vagina.

"Can you explain how we got into this situation in the first place?" Ruth asked. "After all, all of us here are amazing, intelligent, informed women. How do we get into situations like these—even though we all have a good head on our shoulders, we simply don't know to say no and find ourselves tensing up in sexual settings?"

"The gap between our beauty and fabulousness and our ability to conduct our sexuality through genuine, honest attentiveness and communication is quite astounding," I said. "My feeling is that part of it is founded and based on the relationship pattern of slave and master. After all, what is the role of a handmaiden?" I asked.

"Submissive to the master," said Ruth. "She does everything he wants, from a position of servitude, degradation, and not taking a stand. She will capitulate her own needs in the face of his desires. I know this from my own life in so very many forms. It's not just a compliant vagina, but a life full of appeasement. It's simply awful. I can't believe that I have lived this way in so many areas of my life, even in the hospital," Ruth said in a sad voice.

"That's why we're here," I answered, "to conduct our own inquiries, to discover new ways of being and to venture away from these personal and collective patterns." I looked into Ruth's eyes and with a look of love and support I said: "I know that you can do this, and I also know there will be moments where you feel that you can't. We are human, animals on the cyclical wheel of life. One moment, we are at the peak of our lives and in another, we simply want to die. It's OK, death is part of life. When we allow parts of ourselves to die, there will be space for renewal and for new revelations. That's the process. It happens for everyone at exactly the right pace for them, and it's just as it should be!

"The pattern of master and slave is encoded in society and resides in relationships between man and woman. It may manifest itself with the man as the master and the woman as the slave, or the woman as the mistress and the man, the servant."

"Wow, I never thought of it like that," said Ellie. "What you're saying is absolutely awful. It's a constant power play. Essentially, women subjugate their men, too, and then they themselves become their servants."

"It's an ego game, for both slave and master. The master takes energy, uses his authority with force and demands subjection through power, authority, threat, and fear. The submissive slave gives in, not from desire, but from fear. The mistress takes over, imposing her authority, emasculating the man, and he gives from a place of his diminished status, not from desire nor inner power. Situations like these flow from fear or from misinformation about how life should be in balance between the forces of male-female," I said.

"What do you mean by in the male-female?" asked Beth.

"The masculine has more linear, unambiguous, and astute characteristics," I said. "We all know these qualities within ourselves. The feminine, meanwhile, is rounder, softer, containing, slow, and intuitive. Every single one of us, women and men, are mixed and built from these two virtues. The more we learn to respect them, to be connected with them, and to collaborate between them, the more we will be able to realize more of who we are, from a place of wholeness and inner happiness."

"So, is it all inside us? Not divided between men and women?" asked Ember.

"Yes," I answered. "I believe that when these forces inside myself are in harmony, in cooperation and clear communication between themselves, the harmony will also be reflected in relations with my partner. When we make changes from the inside, we will know the change has taken root when we begin to see it within our closest relationships."

"I am a senior doctor," said Ruth, who was slouching. "People come to see me from all over the world, but when it comes to my own bedroom, I become compliant, subservient to the master. I don't say what I want, I don't enjoy it, I just do what I have to do for it to be over," she shared bravely.

"Thank you for that intimate confidence," I said. "What you're describing is very common. I meet intelligent women in senior positions, but when it comes to their relationship with the man they live with, they shed that skin and become an obedient slave to their masters. Many of us have been in situations where penetration took place that we didn't really want or, in any case, didn't say no to. Sometimes we don't really feel like doing it or maybe you simply needed a few more minutes until the lingam entered you, but you didn't say so and felt that you didn't have a choice about it. In each such occasion, the vagina contracts, closes, hardens, and is frightened, not freely communicating her desires calmly."

"When will women agree to love and respect our vaginas?" asked Ember in frustration.

"When women dare tell the man in front of them that they don't want it to be this way! I'm not willing to go along with it anymore in my life, but many times, despite being fully aware of it, I have found myself in sexual situations I didn't know how to stop in time," said Ember agitatedly.

"It's a process," I said and I took a deep breath. I felt the accumulated tension in the body, sensing submission and helplessness. I felt the feeling build up inside me as though I were enduring the submissive experiences of all the women present.

I flicked my eyes towards the window and I saw a small hummingbird darting between the water droplets. I felt happy at the sight of it. The bird reminded me of the choice to live a happy life, the ability to be free and to flit and float amid an endless number of things.

"It's a process of deep cleansing," I continued, "that calls for a lot of patience on the way. It takes time to free oneself of the patterns of doing something unwillingly for the masculine energy and to demand respect for the female sexual being. Honor the crevice or hole, the orifice, the feminine[5] , the spring of life that we are—a life of respect and in harmony with the masculine side that also exists inside us and knows how to be explicit and unequivocal—bring down the light and higher knowledge from above, be organized and accomplished. This is an all-inclusive being of a woman who empowers both the masculine and feminine within her, so they may be balanced and companions on the road.

"As to your question, Ember, I feel that it's already happening. The very fact that we are sitting here is already indicative of change. Every woman who has taken a step to find equilibrium between the masculine and feminine not only becomes an inspiration, but also awakens the possibility of more people having the opportunity to choose, if only by virtue of her presence.

"It's a universal responsibility for each one of us to engage in the deep processes to face and integrate our sexual energy, which can free us from ancient patterns of silence and subservience, to inspire men and women to instigate change in their lives, to find balance between the male and the female, and to learn to conduct themselves from a place of happiness and pleasure from their sexual energy."

I saw that Iris was sitting awkwardly and asked her: "Is there something I can clarify for you?"

"What you are talking about makes sense when it's between a man and a woman," she said, "but to see them as inner parts

---

5. In Hebrew, the word for feminine, 'nekeva,' also means a creek, a water source; and contains the word 'nekev,' meaning hole or crevice.

of ourselves is a bit of a stretch for me and I just can't manage to catch on to what you mean."

I searched inside myself for help from the Creator to find the clearest, most precise words. "What I mean is that both masculine and feminine forces exist within us all. You cannot fully give your gift to the world if you don't know how to let go and let the world come into you. If you are afraid, if you shirk away, if your body is clenched, or perhaps you don't receive support, it's fair to assume that you will not be able to give your gifts to the world to your full power and ability. What we're talking about is a balanced relationship between giving and receiving, so that you can at once be penetrated and also penetrate the world. In other words, you shall enter into the world and allow the world to enter you. The ability to let go and allow entry is a feminine quality, while the ability to enter is a masculine value. Our lives may flourish when the attributes of both of them work together in unison, mutual respect, devotion, and with the capacity to rely on one another," I said and I saw that the hummingbird was mid-flight. I felt the magic of the moment within me as the women enthusiastically drank in the knowledge that came through me.

"Let's take a ten-minute break. Make yourselves a hot drink, go to the bathroom, and come back to sit in the circle." I prepared myself a warm cup of cacao and when I went back to sit down, I observed the small, intimate groups that had formed amongst the women. My heart was full of happiness. After a few minutes, all of them had returned to their places and surprisingly, after little more than ten minutes, we continued.

"We have discussed the patterns of victimhood and the patterns of needing to please that create contractions in the vagina and actually create contractions in life all round. Does anyone have any more questions or musings on this topic?" I asked.

"Michal," said Carol, who was sitting upright. Carol had a remarkable presence that magnetized you towards her the moment she began to speak.

"I haven't spoken until now," she said. "I am taking what you are saying now and adding another layer, one that is not necessarily a sexual encounter, but more like what happens when the forces of male and female that exist within me meet. I do agree that more respect, dependence, and camaraderie would help strengthen relations between the male and female. But I want to share something I identify within myself. When I do something or act with decisiveness, parts of me totally trust myself and what I'm doing, but simultaneously, harsh criticism also comes up within me, voices that don't believe me, don't trust my confidence or my decisiveness. And vice versa. In moments where I relax and do nothing, I almost always inevitably shame myself for it, blaming myself for resting and allowing myself to do nothing. In short, my diagnosis is I have more of a struggle going on inside me than there is any dependence, cooperation, or harmony. "

*I choose to learn and live life in balance,*
*harmony, collaboration, and respect*
*between the masculine and feminine*
*energies that reside within me.*

"Thank you, Carol," I said, full of gratitude for the clear way Carol had expressed the complex depth between contradictory forces and these life dynamics.

"Your words have basically brought us to the next topic that explains how we got into this situation in the first place, a world that validates patterns of both overt and covert struggles between the sexes. This is a war of existence, a war about power. Within such a patriarchal society, there may be constant attempts to prove that the male forces are more significant than the female ones," I continued. "There is a lack of appreciation in our society for quiet, soft, slow movement. In our society, success is measured according to male criteria,

not female. Similarly, men are not given legitimacy to express feminine energy, softness, or sensitivity. They are not applauded for creating life. On the other hand, women are demanded to prove they have the right to exist and therefore often quash their valuable feminine gifts; they are not given a place to flourish, they are neither appreciated nor respected. Do you know this feeling?" I asked.

"Of course," said Ruth and all the other women nodded in agreement.

"Men also feel the need to prove their 'masculinity,'" I continued, "and this obligation to prove themselves creates struggle and fear—from abandonment, from crying, from love, from partnership, from living with full power and full implementation of their true potential; fear from a life in peace. I am going to share my own private and personal story with you," I continued. "My partner and I went through something that may arouse inspiration for men and women as one. Exactly one year ago, my friend, a sister for all intents and purposes, sat across from me, looked at me straight in the eye, in full love and genuine care for me, and reflected to me that I am in a couple that wasn't supporting me at all. She told me that the relationship no longer matches with who I am today and that I am more suited to share a life with a man who is present, powerful, and fulfilled." I took a deep breath. Until now, I had only shared this story with my closest friends. I felt the heat in my body rise and as I began to sweat and tremble with fear, I surrendered to confiding this story. It was about time to bring to light the knowledge this story brings.

"My first response to her words was to breathe deeply. Every cell in my body knew that she was reflecting a painful truth to me. I told her thank you. For my 44th birthday, that was the gift I was given—a painful truth straight to the gut. I took responsibility and dove into the work of reorganizing my energy, our energies, anew.

We have three children together. Getting up and leaving was a possibility, but I felt that I hadn't made enough genuine effort yet to just go and break apart our home. I understood that the reasons why we met 14 years ago were no longer relevant; both of us were in a different place now. It was about time to meet in a new place.

"The first thing that was clearly the right thing to do was to truly separate the energy between us. For three months, we would sleep in different rooms. We didn't make love and almost never touched one another physically. Throughout the three months, we expected anger to come up, and it did: anger that hadn't come out over the years; anger I didn't even know was there in the first place. I was angry, I fought, I released and shed the accumulated pain of years and maybe even generations of women. I walked around with enormous rage. The only thing that did manage to calm me down was to observe our children. I told myself that they were amazing, and, therefore, it was fair to think there are probably amazing seeds rooted in the encounter between myself and the man that I lived with.

"One of the first things I did was to sit and write my intentions for how the man I live with should look. I read them to him and his response was: in your dreams. That will never happen. But I stood my ground. It didn't matter to me. I knew clearly that this was no longer an option!

"I knew that it was very important I get acquainted with myself without him being in my energetic space, and that he will get acquainted with himself without me in his energetic space. The fact that we chose to sleep separately really supported that process, so slowly, but surely, I began to loosen my grip on the rigid intentions I had placed on who he is and how the man I live with should be, how he should behave and act in the world. Instead, I went inside. I realized that I wanted to stand more in my own power, to be wilder, to be more alive, more fulfilled, more able to rest, more of a mother, more relaxed, more satisfied with life, and to bring more light into the world. At the same time, in all honesty, all I really felt like doing was to lay down and die, to get into bed, and definitely not to guide some workshop or ceremony. My body instructed me to rest. And so, I came down with a flu that took me a month to get over and, on top of that, hemorrhoids that exhausted my very being for four entire months. Shockingly, all the while, I was undertaking an inner investigation. I understood that I had created this reality myself: the reality that I live with a man who I had castrated with my own hands and he, from his side, cooperated with me by not really feeling castrated. I belittled him, in truth, because I was scared, afraid to death that he would be great, huge, and powerful."

"Wait, stop," said Ember. "You are so brave! Essentially what you are saying is that you were afraid to be with a powerful man because you were afraid that he would belittle you or challenge you too much, but basically, by doing that, you only made yourself smaller and didn't stand in your own power."

"Correct," I continued, "because if I live next to a huge, great, powerful man, he will simply control me, kill me, and not allow me to be who I am. So, I killed him first. I ruled with an iron fist. I am powerful, I am in charge, managing the home, the domestic finances, I am paying the bills, fixing the punctured tires, bringing in the money, managing the children's education, the children's pediatrics. In short, everything that could be managed I would manage and everything was under my control. No man was a match for me. Except for the fact that the masculine side within me was burnt out and could no longer continue like that. The feminine inside of me was afraid all the time, afraid that she would be killed, so from the start she killed herself. The woman of the house turned into a man and the man turned to a softness that was unbalanced and unsupported.

"Within all of that, slowly, but diligently, something inside of me began to choose to be a woman in partnership with a man. A woman who trusted, who led in partnership, who studied and taught, who loosened her grip, who let go, who learned lessons and attracted abundance."

"What does that mean, to attract abundance?" asked Iris.

"The art of attracting abundance is one of the expressions of the feminine energy," I said. "Maybe we'll discuss that later. That's a workshop in and of itself.

"From the crisis of living in such a reality that I had carved out for myself with my own hands, I decided that I now choose differently!

"I decided to envisage that I live in peace with my inner power and that, next to me, there was a man who lives in his own presence and power. I imagined that I am confident next to him and him next to me; that I trust in him and he trusts in me; that I want to talk and to share with him in the depths that I dive into myself and to dive in bravely together with him; and that I succeed in doing that. I visualized that I gave consent for my partner to enter deeply into the depths of my soul and my existence. My soul was already yearning for this. We decided to get closer. It felt so very strange that he was touching me again. Suddenly, we didn't know how to touch each other. Everything felt new, like our souls were asking to meet. A year has gone by since that earthquake. Something new has sprouted. There was deep conversation and we became so very close, so much so that there is now a 'home' in my house. When we hug, the hug is deep, all-enveloping, ever-present, loving. There is now a woman in me who has agreed to control the world a little less and to be in it a little more; and a man who has agreed to give more of his gifts to the world. I have masculine energy in me that agrees to give and a feminine energy in me that agrees to let go—and the two of them cooperate with each other!

"Yet, even with all that I have gone through in my relationship between the male and female inside me, I still feel I have more to learn, to deepen, and to grow from this mutual partnership. This is a walk with so many challenges and brave choices to make; and can only be done through respectful collaboration between these two forces."

"Wow," said Ember. "You're so brave!"

"I was in a relationship for almost 40 years," said Beth, "and I wasn't brave enough to say these things to myself, let alone to my husband.

It's so wonderful that you did that. My husband was a wonderful man. I controlled him with a firm hand and if he didn't do as I asked, he was in trouble. What you did is so inspiring, but how does one even go about doing that? Weren't you afraid that you would break up?"

"I almost died from pure terror," I answered, smiling, "but then, by that point, I simply couldn't continue anymore regardless. I had to change the very foundation of our partnership. Perhaps it's more accurate to say that both of us had to do it, because he, too, was no longer happy in his place."

Suddenly, Ruth began to cry. From time to time, she tried to talk, but every word that came out caused an additional bout of tears. The girls moved in closer to her and Ellie got up and brought her a tissue. Ruth wiped her nose; her face was pink and her eyes red. After a little while, her crying subsided and Ruth began to talk. "You have opened a long-held wound for me. The separation from my husband hurt me so much. I had so wanted us to succeed to stay together, but it simply didn't work. I didn't have the guts and neither of us dared to look inside ourselves. Not to mention the idea of updating our relationship to match who we are 20 years after we married, as both of us were already different people..."

"Ruth love," I said, "it's time to dive inside, to peel off the layers and evolve from the lesson you received from the separation. We tend to recreate the same relationships even with new people. Therefore, the more you dare to break free from the patterns that no longer serve you— both in the relationship with yourself and with the men in your life—the greater chance you will have for something new to form inside of you; and that will become evident and reflected in the relationships in your life!" I looked at her and asked: "Do you consent to clear the patterns that prevent you from living? Do you agree to heal the pain from the separation and allow yourself a life of more happiness and pleasure?"

She looked at me and said: "I really want that, but I simply don't know how, what to do, or even why bother doing it. We are not together anymore and that hurts me so much." As she spoke, tears flowed, washing her face. Ellie placed a hand on her upper back, behind her heart.

Beth looked at her and said: "Ruth, my husband has passed away and it's a little like a separation. Behold, I have a new relationship and here I am with a dry vagina that stops me from having a sexual relationship. But thanks to that, I woke up and came to this workshop. Look what a beautiful woman you are. It seems to me that you will find a wonderful man to be by your side, but it's worthwhile that first you will have time by yourself to take care of yourself. You came here, so you're already heading in the right direction." Beth looked at her with compassion. Ruth wiped her last few tears with a tissue and calmed down a little from Beth's comforting words.

"I am so very afraid to change," she said. "What if I won't recognize myself and don't know who I am?"

I looked at her with love and before I could even answer her, Ellie said: "But what is that fear? The fear of changing our ways. Why is it so hard to change?"

I looked sensitively at Ruth, checking with her wordlessly if it was OK for me to continue. I got a look of agreement and I answered Ellie:

"That's a very important point to perceive — the fear — and what happens to us when we are in fear? Let's go back to the breath," I said. I felt that I had spoken a lot and the participants were listening to me, from outside of themselves. What was important for me was to teach how to perform inner listening. First of all, with the breath and inner observation; and then the outer response to the world from a more centered, clearer, and lighter place.

"Place your hands on your vaginal area," I requested. "Now breathe into her, consent to being friends with her. Take your breath down through the opening of the vaginal canal and then empty it of the air slowly. And again—inhale to where your vagina is and into its opening. Allow the breath to be fuller. When we breathe into our base, we are also utilizing the inflation of the lungs more and they grant deeper entry into the body and soul. Empty the air out. Again, take another breath of air and then hold your breath, gently and calmly relaxing your body, staying with your awareness of your vaginal area. Great. Be with her, be with yourselves. Feel that with every breath, she is receiving from you, she is expanding and growing when you give her space, conscious space, and awakening your lives from within. At the same time as you deep-breathe, ask your vagina how she is. Let go of your inner critic. Just listen to her with all your senses and she will answer you."

The room was quiet, silent with a hint of exploration and discovery. Women of a wide variety of ages were sitting in a circle together by choice, breathing into their vaginas, and, moreover, practicing listening, asking after the wellbeing of their vaginas. Only the sound of breathing could be heard in the room. Slowly, as if conjured by magic, everyone's breathing became unified, creating one rhythmic, singular breath, the common beat of breathing in sync, hallelujah!

"Notice what is happening within you, ladies," I said. "Notice the softness that is unfolding from within in attunement with your breath. That softness is our gift, a gift to take with you as you walk your path in cooperation with the Earth. Talk to your vaginas, ask her what she, your soft vagina, goes through when you are afraid? Please remain soft right now. Do not fear. Ask your soft vagina."

I saw the tension that appeared on Embar and Carol's faces and I said: "Relax your jaws and your mouth. When your mouth is slack, so, too, is your vagina. They are a part of the same muscular system that affects one and other. Relax your eyes and forehead, great. Pay attention to how the body facilitates and relaxes immediately when the face is loose. Keep asking the vagina what happens to her when she is afraid."

I gave the women a few minutes to observe inside and continued: "When a clear picture or maybe a word, sound, or feeling comes up in your mind's eye, please share it with us out loud—all the while keeping your eyes closed."

There were a few moments of silence and then, Noa said quietly: "Shriveling."

Iris added, "Blocked."

Ember said: "Lays armor on me, armor on my vagina and also on my heart."

"I am sorry, but no words, nothing is coming up for me," Ruth said apologetically.

"It's OK," I encouraged. "It's possible to connect to feelings without words, too."

"Curling up inside like a turtle," said Beth.

"The word dehydrated comes up for me," said Ellie.

"When I feel fear," said Carol, "I want to protect myself and to defend myself, sometimes the way I do that is to really go to war over something." She hesitated for a moment, adding, "Maybe it's not exactly coming from my vagina, but more from my head."

"That's good," I said, "thank you, all of you, for sharing. You can show gratitude to your vagina for sharing her sensitivities with you. We will take a few breaths here from the mouth and release a sigh momentarily. Sighing, as I mentioned before, is one of the most advantageous tools we must release overloads of surplus energy."

The room filled with the sound of releasing sighs. I observed them and noticed that for some women, it was very easy to open their voices and for others it was very hard. I felt that in order to be able to continue speaking about fear and what it brings, we

75

needed to shake out our bodies and release sounds to clear out our systems.

"Come, let us return to talking about fear and how it affects us. Many people react to fear by struggling or declaring war, perhaps from a sincere and authentic intention to protect themselves. As all of us know, the vast majority of women in the world carry the memories and recollections of fearing men, especially regarding sexuality. Men who penetrate their space without permission. But men, too, hold memories of pain and fear from women regarding sexuality. To protect ourselves, we closed ourselves off and built a system of armor that protects us well, especially around the pelvis. You can call it the chastity belt. Our society is composed of so many people who wear thick armor to guard and protect themselves. The armor blocks the energetic flow of the natural way of life. The pace of life is disrupted and we experience life in opposition to nature and our personal rhythm.

"As a result, we feel frustrated and dissatisfied. Many people with so much tremendous potential feel small; they are unrealized and unfulfilled. It's fair to assume that the first place where our frustration comes out is at home, towards our partner. We fight with one another over our place, status, and worth. Many women behave disrespectfully and aggressively control their partners. Simultaneously, many men behave disrespectfully and controllingly towards their partners. They create a dependent relationship without balance, full of great pain, lack of respect, and lack of love.

"Distrust, covert hatred, and disrespect are encoded in the way that men and women are treating each other. We forget how to be balanced on the ground. We forget the essence, the knowledge of a shared movement between men and women coming from a place of respect and living together in harmony. We forget to support each other and to remember we are part of the one wholeness.

*In full presence, in peace and in partnership
with the Creator, I am choosing and
learning to live a life of peace and harmony
with the masculine energy that is inside me
and alongside the men in my life.*

# WHY EMPOWER AND RELAX YOUR VULVA?

After a short break, all of us returned to sit down.

"We spoke earlier of how we managed to get into this situation in the first place; how we managed to create a society where so many women in the world walk around with a clenched vagina. Now, I invite us to investigate why it is worthwhile for us to relax and empower the vagina. Why should we even want to do such a thing?

"But first, I want to explain the infinity pattern that can be represented by a geometric shape ∞. It is a powerful symbol in which its conscious use grants us qualities of balance, communication, and the transformation of present energy to be integrated into the material, into our daily lives. The infinity transmits information from place to place. At the point in its middle, the point of connection in the confluence between the two circles, the magic happens. I recommend you trace and flow the infinity pattern inside yourself and between the people around you. It will support and deepen the opportunity for clear connection between people. Today, we will use it to set in motion and flow information between the heart and the vulva, the throat and the vulva, and the third eye and the vulva. This is done to permit clear communication between your vulva and the rest of your body. Any questions?"

"I didn't understand any of that," said Beth. "How am I supposed to flow a pattern of infinity from me to other people?"

"I didn't get it either," added Ruth. "I don't understand what 'tracing a pattern of infinity' means. It's as though you spoke Chinese to me right now."

"Thank you all for bringing me back down to Earth," I laughed. "Sometimes I really speak too abstractly. In essence, in our core, we are energy and, therefore, we react to energy quickly. Energy is a wave, like in the sea. It's the most fun thing to play in the waves, right? I invite us to play, to inspire, and to manage our personal energy deliberately and consciously. One of the material expressions of energy is electricity. The infinity pattern allows the electricity of your energetic body to flow better within the energetic network." In the room, I felt there was a lack of understanding, but at the same time, I knew there was a wave of curiosity awakening. It was clear to me that Ember and Ellie understood what I was referring to, but the rest of the women in the room had no idea or familiarity with the energetic contents that I was bringing.

"Maybe you have heard certain words and terms for the first time here that perhaps aren't clear to you as to how they are connected to an empowered vulva. I will try to explain. To want to free and relax our vulva, it is on us to choose to stand in our full power. To do this, we must bravely overcome fear. To accomplish this important mission, it is worthwhile to use our gifts that the universe gave to us humans to be able to live in our power and be a radiant body of light, strength, and power. One of the fields that I studied is the technique of electromagnetic balance—EMF Balancing Technique®. Therefore, I know that as we improve our conductivity within the energetic network that surrounds us, that inimitable spark can materialize as matter. When we learn to use the infinity pattern that surrounds us, and is also present in our physical bodies, in a conscious way, our communication with ourselves and with our surroundings becomes clearer and is much improved.

"The more you choose to practice it, the more you will feel, the greater the effect of the infinity patterns. Experience it and learn from those experiences. We can use it through the power of imagination, the power of the senses, the power of thought, and through the power of feeling energy."

In the background, we could hear the sound of raindrops pattering on the roof of the yurt, creating different beats, each time a different stroke and movement. Between the clouds, rays of winter sunshine peeped out as a beautiful afternoon light filtered through the window. All at once, as if we had turned on another light in the room, each and everyone's heart was lit up. They all looked to the window as a golden light washed over the room. Just as I had spoken of the body of light that radiates brightly, the sun reminded us that even from within the gray, sunlight that completely changes the way things appear could suddenly burst forth and provide a wide range of colors and shades.

"I love it so much when we are given a clear sign that the universe is talking to us and supporting us in our journey on Earth," I said. "Come now, let's take a deep breath of glorious golden sun. Place one hand on the vaginal area and the other on the heart and simply breathe deep breaths. Inhale air through the nose and exhale out the mouth. When we inhale, use your imaginations to guide the air down to the vaginal opening. When we breathe out, allow the infinity pattern of eight to flow between the vulva and the heart, with the center, the eight, situated near the naval. Allow the pattern of eight to flow from the heart to the vulva and from the vulva back to the heart, at your own pace. It can be fast or it can be slow. It can also be synchronized with the breath, but it doesn't have to be. Allow the movement within you to form the eight and to flow from you, unleashing the rhythm and control.

"With the breath, sexuality and love flows between the heart and the vulva. Sexuality comes up into the heart and love flows down into the vulva. I invite you to place the intention to connect between the heart and the vulva, to deepen the connection and conversation with your vulva." I asked the women to say out loud what they felt physically from the conscious movement of the infinity pattern between the heart and the vulva. The answers we received were diverse: A fast heartbeat; awakened sexuality; flowing of energy; movement; that something is flowing there that feels new to me; heat in the hands; feeling my entire body.

I sensed joy awakening inside me. Usually, I do these processes by myself, experiencing the energy and the movement within my inner world. I was filled with excitement at the privilege of being able to teach these skills. Living with and from an awareness of the energetic body around us gives us strength to live a more powerful, fuller, and fulfilled life.

"Using that connection with your hearts and vulva," I carried on, "I invite you to conduct an internal inquiry as to why it is worthwhile for you to free and empower your vulva. Ask her why you should release your grip. It's going one step further to removing your chastity belt, doing away with the physical and energetic protective blanket that we covered our vulva with throughout the generations. Ask her; sit with the question inside you, between you and your vulva: why is it worth it for me to relax and empower you?"

Silence fell upon the space. I thought about the fact that since time immemorial, women have dreamed of being in their power on Earth, but equally have also avoided it. Throughout history, it has been dangerous for women to fully bring themselves. In many places in the world, they were hunted down and burned for being midwives and healers. This memory remains encoded within our feminine network and we have avoided creating a life that expresses ourselves as fully as the lights we are. For many women, avoidance of our light has created deep pain.

At this moment of grace, an opportunity was created to allow more women to march away from their past, to cross the threshold towards something new in their lives. I allowed the energy to flow between my heart and my vulva a while, strengthening this picture and my intentions for all those present. I felt that, despite the difficulty some of the women were experiencing, each one, in her own unique way, was consenting to connect to the wholeness, the entirety of her personal energy, and thus allowing herself to be more of who she is.

"My vulva and my heart both told me...," started Ember after some time had passed, "that it is worth relaxing and empowering my vulva because then it will be easier to release the things that overload me and sit inside my pelvis.

"What do you mean?" asked Beth.

"Are you asking me or my vulva?" laughed Ember. "It's basically the same thing." She closed her eyes and stayed with her hands over her vaginal area and her heart and continued: "I will give you the answer that comes up for me from my rather chatty vulva. My pelvis is overloaded with tension built up over all the times that I didn't say no when what was happening didn't suit me. Not only during sex, but also in life in general. My pelvis is packed with an existential and primal fear. There are few places where I feel truly at home and comfortable. Layers of tension have been piling up from each time that I didn't feel that way. To empower the vulva is to release the existential and basic fear that someone may come and rape me anytime they like."

"I also feel fear from my vagina that I might be raped, and that triggers me without me even being aware of it," said Ellie.

"I remind you to focus on why we want to relax and empower the vulva. Ask your vulva: why is it worth it to empower her?"

"My vulva said," said Ellie, "that it is really, really worthwhile for me to let go of the fear of being raped. I just don't know how."

"We'll get to that later," I said. "You're bringing up the memory from this life and from generations and generations of women who have experienced male penetration without consent. Clearing this root pain will pave the way for a different future for our daughters. Come, let's continue to breathe authentically with as little filter as possible and ask: why should I empower my vulva?"

"My vagina," said Iris, "is a gateway to life and wants to give birth easily."

"Correct, it is absolutely easier to give birth through an empowered vagina," I confirmed. "She is a soft, happy, and more relaxed gate that allows the fetus to pass through her more easily and calmly.

"I feel more power, more energy flowing within me," said Ruth, "so I guess freeing and empowering the vulva gives me more power and energy."

"I will definitely be a more relaxed woman if I empower her," said Beth. "So much tension had accumulated inside my body around the subject of men and sexuality over the years. This is the first time in my life that I actually recognize that. That sexual tension constricts my vagina. I hope it's not too late to change all that."

"It's never too late," I replied. "Even coming to this workshop is already a huge step forward." I looked towards the burning flame in the fireplace and I felt gratitude and appreciation to Beth for her bravery at her age to break free from her life patterns and meet other parts of herself.

"The vagina is the most sensual point where we experience our relationships with the world," I said. "Most people are created from the joining of a penis to a vagina and from relationships between a man and a woman. Through the vagina, the world penetrates into us in the most physical and tangible way there can be. For as long as that center will have less tension surrounding it, so, too, will our relationships with the world be less tense."

I stopped to sense the needs within the room. "Lower your hands from your heart and vulva, get up slowly to stand up, and start to sway your hips to the movement of the infinity symbol, making an eight, with your vagina as the center. Imagine a pencil is coming out of your vagina and drawing the eight and the movement will slowly, simply just flow. Breathe deep and full breaths throughout the movement and focus your attention on what is happening...."

"I feel freedom," said Ember enthusiastically.

"My hips feel really stiff and I am barely managing to move," said Iris.

I took the drum and started to beat it. The room filled with the light of the women who moved their hips in the infinity symbol. Some of them found it hard; it was easy for others, but what was clearly visible was their smiles, which slowly formed and widened on their faces.

I increased the rhythm of the drumbeat and happiness, along with a surge of energy of something beginning to get unstuck, filled the room. The beat went faster and faster and all at once, I gave a final stroke and stopped playing, with a huge smile on my face.

I continued to talk. "I wanted you to feel what happens to you when you move your hip in a conscious way. An empowered and free vulva is the key to happiness and to more self-love. She is the gate that agrees to contain love and to pass on love from the spirit world, the world that dreams up and brings a soul or a creation into the material world. The vagina is the convergent gate between the spirit and the material.

"Sit back down, close your eyes once more, and imagine yourselves in an act of love in a space that is hard for you to fully relax into, perhaps because it is noisy or there is an outside disturbance that doesn't support you. Imagine that you are uncomfortable, feel or sense yourselves starting to constrict and cramp up. Maybe you aren't even aware that you're clenching because your thoughts have wandered in other directions. Your partner touches you in a way that is not quite right for you; your body understands that, but it doesn't manage to obtain full awareness of the fact and maybe you aren't willing to put it into words. Observe; see in your mind's eye what is happening to your vulva, what happens to the other parts of your body, what happens to your soul. Is it nice to experience sexual encounters where you are cramping up? How does this pattern serve you? Be with the answers inside yourselves, breathe deeply, be with the authentic feeling that is situated right now inside your body. Great."

The room was silent and I returned to drumming a steady beat. After a few minutes, I moved on to play the Tibetan singing bowls. I asked everyone to lie down on their backs or on their sides, relax their bodies, and allow them to sink into earth.

"Release the muscles in your face. When your face is relaxed, your vaginas can relax more easily, too. The jaw muscles influence the vagina. The circular muscles of the mouth and of the vagina are attached with a direct line. When you laugh, the vagina laughs; when you are tense, the vagina tenses; when you are angry, the vagina is angry." I spoke in a calm and relaxed demeanor, allowing more softness and tranquility to reverberate inside my physical body.

"I am asking you to relax your jaws, to take off the edge of your tongue from touching the roof of your mouth, with your mouth slightly open and the lower jaw slightly dropped down. Great. Your body is quiet and relaxed. I invite you to imagine, to sense, to feel yourselves making love. You are situated in a physically supportive space, in a charming environment. There is quiet all around you; all the external conditions are aligned to allow and support you surrendering to the act of love. Your body is soft and relaxed, there is pleasurable intimacy with your partner, and every part of you is melting. When something doesn't feel nice, you say so; your body signals what does and doesn't suit you. Your partner for love-making is attentive to you. Notice how your vagina feels. What is going on with her?"

I continued to sound the Tibetan singing bowls. The rain began to fall again, sounding a new thudding rhythm. The melody of the bowls merged with the melody of the rain as though creating a graceful moment of unity and harmony reminiscent of the merging of the sacred and harmonious potential between man and woman, between masculine and feminine. When there is attentiveness and harmony, the water knows where to flow, the sounds merge, and the breath becomes one. The gates of creation open; it is all one. I finished sounding on the bowls and I took the drum and quietly and gently drummed the rhythm of a heartbeat. I drummed a steady, constant rhythm that reminds us of the heartbeat of the Earth that bestows upon us life, strength, and the desire to fulfill who we truly are, in every component of the whole being that composes who we are; through the heart, the head, the stomach, the throat, the hands, the feet, and the vagina.

"Please bring your awareness to the here and now," I requested, "and listen to the beat: of the drum, the beat of your heart, the one and only, unparalleled in all the world."

I waited a few moments to allow them to deepen their inner listening to their hearts and continued: "What was the difference between a released vagina and a constricted vagina? Where was it more pleasant and safer for you? Where do you want to lead yourselves in your relationships with your vaginas and essentially with the world? The vagina, like the mouth, experiences relationships with the world in the most physical manner. Food enters the mouth, the penis enters the vagina and nourishes us, feeds us. The word in Sanskrit for the male genitalia is *lingam,* meaning 'rod of light.' The role of the penis is to illuminate love in the vagina. Rods of light illuminate the womb, the Gate of Creation. Beloved women, what do you choose to feed you? The way of the empowered and relaxed vulva that agrees to be nourished, or the way of the constricted, clenched vulva?"

Together with the constant beat of the drum, I began to sing in a high and quivering voice, in a frequency that would reach deep into the cells of the body, awakening and stimulating new life forces, shining light on parts of the soul that had lain dormant. Playing the drum,[6] spontaneously, the following poem flowed through me:

"Empowered vulva, empowered vulva,

------------------

6. In Hebrew, the word 'tof' means drum, which, if you reverse the letters, is 'pot,' which means vulva in Hebrew.

87

agree to receive the gift of creation.
empowered vulva, Empowered vulva,
agree to receive the gift of creation.
Awaken, Awaken, from the depths of your being,
Come be connected to me,
Be close to me,
Whisper to me,
The secret of creation."

The words and the music repeated for over ten minutes. One by one, the women joined in singing with me. Magic, harmony, and unity pervaded the room. The song ended. The room was silent and Ember sighed and said: "This is how I want to make love, while I feel this kind of connection, this harmony, this unity. Without words, everything is in sync. I so love to feel this simplicity, the godliness that is present in everything."

Happiness arose in my heart from what Ember had voiced. I held an inner smile and continued to talk: "Stay as you are, lying or sitting down, everyone in their comfortable positions. Rest your palms and lovingly nourish the parts of you that are requesting your attention."

Ellie rested her hands on her heart, Ember on her lower abdomen, Beth, on her face. I gave them a few moments of quiet before continuing to speak.

"Nourish yourselves with love. The more you know about how to give yourselves and agree to receive love from yourselves, the greater your ability to receive love from outside will grow. Self-love is the key to a healthy life. One of the expressions of love is that you take responsibility for your choices and invite into your lives sexual connections that deepen your ties to unity and to creation. It is worthwhile to release and empower the vulva because it deepens your connection to G-d, to Creation, to unity, to the universe, to magic, or however you want to refer to it. Everyone has their own word and understanding. When the vulva is empowered, relaxed, released, and openly voicing her desires, a direct line will be opened to connecting with creation, and when we connect to creation, our lives become easier, more meaningful, and deeper.

"You're basically saying that if we will believe in G-d, we will have a more pleasurable sex life?" Carol asked.

"A powerful energy of creation flows from everything, within each one of us and the entire universe," I said with a smile. "The ability to merge with the creator within the act of love strengthens our sexual encounters and pleasure. The vagina, by being an organ from which new life is created, is therefore sacred. She asks to be treated gently, maybe sometimes with a lot of intensity, but always with a lot of attention and love. Each part of the female reproductive system—the vagina, the vaginal canal, the fallopian tubes and the uterus—constitutes a direct gateway to the creator. The very creation of life occurs in the female reproductive organs. The eggs and the sperm meet and allow a new soul to enter the world. Women have the right and the privilege to be in direct contact with the remarkable ability to create life. The act of love exists within the holy of holies of creation of life on Earth."

I fell silent. Sometimes, I feel there is a wisdom and energy of its own in a workshop, a wisdom that conveys the content without words. In parallel to the subjects I discuss, the energy and knowledge that goes inside our body's cells pass wordlessly, intensely, filtering deep into the layers of the DNA of everybody present.

Ruth, who still lay on her mattress, started to speak. "This entire process surprises me. When you described the first scenario, I felt the tension that reverberated in my body, bringing up so much discomfort and insecurity. For me, to relax is one of the scariest things there is. I normally make sure I am in control all the time. To my surprise, it was precisely during the relaxation part that I felt a surge of so much power, beyond what I have ever known before, not to mention during an act of love. I was really surprised that it was actually in the act of relaxing that I discovered my inner strength!"

"Thank you, Ruth. What you shared with us is really important," I said and I asked everyone who was still lying down to sit up. One by one, the women got up. It seemed like everyone present had gone through a meaningful experience. The rain had let up and the last orange-red light of the end of the day shone into the room. I was relaxed, paying constant attention to the feeling of tranquility in the room and wellbeing of the women in the workshop. I felt that most of the participants had gone through a significant experience, although I wasn't sure how Noa was doing. I felt that her silence hid an inner storm. I prayed that every one of the participants' experiences had been embedded within the cells of their bodies and would become realized and used in their daily lives. I prayed the women would have more courage to be who they truly are. I thought about my own life journey where I had crossed through the gates of so many fears—I trembled from them—but from that place, armed with a lot of courage, I had learned and I am still learning to be daring, to keep connecting, and to strive to fulfill myself in my entirety and in my full power in my everyday existence. It was time for a break.

"I want to ask you all that when you go to the bathroom to urinate and to relieve yourselves, do it with the intention that with this urine, you will rid yourself of the fear of your own power," I said, and with that, the women left for a break.

The sun was already beginning to set. I opened the window to let into the space some fresh, new air. One by one, the women got up, made tea, got out their sandwiches, and ate or left to go outside to get air. Quiet prevailed, a peaceful silence, serene and deep while everyone was still digesting what they had gone through.

Suddenly in the room, I heard Ruth's low voice addressing Ember, asking: "Can I have a hug?"

Ember acceded to her request, opening her arms and enveloping

Ruth with her soft, thin body. Ruth sank in her arms and into the hug that existed outside of time and space. Ruth relaxed and a feeling of serenity appeared to arise inside of her. It was clear to me that Ruth wasn't used to such hugs and Ember knew that; and Ember's incredible tenderness managed to dissolve the walls of Ruth's heart and body. Ember let go of Ruth and they looked into each other's eyes. Ruth's eyes shone and Ember's good heart smiled straight into her eyes, and in a fraction of a second, more layers of pain and stubbornness of the heart melted away for both of them. When the heart of one opens, it immediately affects the other person in their proximity and will soften them from inside and allow more loving energy to flow more easily and freely in the space.

"Thank you," said Ruth. "I have never had a hug like that before."

"Yes, I know," said Ember, "and I am happy to be the first to be privileged to get such a hug from you, with so much love and softness. May many people be lucky enough to get a hug from you."

Then, I saw Carol come out from the toilet. Her eyes were twinkling. I heard her, in a relatively quiet voice, enthuse to Ember: "I was in the toilet. I remembered Michal's instruction, which I thought quite strange, to do a wee with the intention of peeing out all the fear. In my life, I never did anything like that. But it was nice and felt empowering!" I was delighted.

*I choose, I inquire within myself, while connecting to my heart, why I should empower and relax my vulva.*

# WHAT IS AN EMPOWERED WOMAN?

When break-time was over, I called the women to return together to the sharing circle. They returned calmly and sat down.

I asked them to rest their hands on their vaginal area and breathe into her once more. Something about having done the action so many times throughout the day already made it easier for them, and this seemed more available and accessible—because every woman breathed and succeeded in deepening her breaths more to the base of the pelvis.

"First of all, beloveds, I want to thank you all. I feel we have a very special environment here; an ease has been woven into the connections between us and I am really happy about that. So. Why, when the vagina is relaxed and empowered, are we more empowered? What does that even mean, to be in our full power?" I asked.

"I understand," said Ruth, "that to be in my power means allowing softness and being more relaxed to be a more meaningful part of my life. I realized that there are places in my life where I am constricted. I work with so many men around me. It's important to me that they will actually listen and hear what I have to say. It causes me a lot of tension and stress and sometimes also drives me to behave more aggressively and violently. It demands a lot of energy and strength and I feel weak and tense. Relaxed I am certainly not. Maybe if I were softer and more serene, with more inner peace, I would invest less effort and it would be easier for me to simply just be. I think there is even a chance I would have been heard more if I were softer and more relaxed."

"Thank you, Ruth, for sharing," I said. "When you are comfortable in your own skin and company, with the way your body looks, with love for your body and for who you are, you are in your power," I added.

"When my periods stopped, I gained weight," said Beth. "I cannot say, either, that in my youth I loved my body. For so very many years, I would criticize myself over how I looked and now, in addition to all that, I have dryness in my vagina and it's just not comfortable for me to experience sexual touch. Does that mean that I am not in my power? I hold a lot of judgment inside towards my body, a lack of love and anger towards my aging form. Still, despite that, I take care of myself."

"If you judge yourself every day," I said, "you will be angry at yourself that the fluids don't flow during sexual contact. There is almost no way that the fluids will flow when you are not relaxed, if you are stressed, angry, or frustrated.

I have met women who experienced dryness in their vaginas when their menses stopped, yet succeeded to pour from anew the fluid of life in their vaginas. They did it from a place of choosing awareness, a place of inquiry into their sexuality, and from understanding that this is a transitional period. Menopause is a time where the menses ends and we enter another cycle, an internal, deep stage, a stage of life that transports women through the gate of wisdom and understanding. We are initiated into the wisdom of the female tribe, the elders, and also into a different kind of sexuality, one that awakens new parts within us for this part of our lives. When you understand that you are wonderful, too, when your vagina right now is dry and you accept it and love yourself, from that place, you can sow seeds of potential for change in your reality and take steps to create a new reality, so that you are in your own power! You learn to work with movement of the forces of the feminine within you—relaxation, compassion, and acceptance, combined with the forces of the masculine—action, sowing seeds, and clarity."

"Are you telling me to love my vagina when it's dry?" asked Beth. "How is it possible to love it? You can't imagine how frustrated I am deep in my being, each time anew, simply ashamed and aggravated that my body doesn't work like it should."

Ember responded quickly: "Maybe your body needs instructions other than those that you had at 30 years old, so that you will be able to produce wetness and sexual energy in the body and simply no one taught you?"

"Where did you get that from," replied Iris. "Also, I need instructions, too, as I've totally lost my sexual desire."

I really loved that information and inquiry was flowing in such an organic way between the participants. "It looks like we've stumbled upon something," I said before contributing another point of view to the debate. "I want to come back to the frustration that Beth brought here. It's something that a lot of women go through and don't share. To love the parts that don't match the instructions of the book that we know is a meaningful stage in our ability to let go and instigate change towards the reality that we want to create. If, despite the concerns and internal pressure, you manage to let go and free your vagina from that situation, something is going to happen, something will shift. It is a tremendous power to learn and to practice loving parts of us we're not happy with. It can be vaginal dryness, but it can also be breasts that are not the same size, my stomach, my shyness, the constriction inside of me, and so on..."

Beth nodded and the rain began to fall once more. The rain,[7] which connects the sky and the Earth, is a symbol of man's ability to descend in spirit form and manifest into the material. For me, it was a sign and a signal from the universe that sparks of agreement

---

7. Rain in Hebrew is 'geshem' and flows from the same root of the word in Hebrew for realization, manifestation, or fulfillment, 'hagshama.'

had been awakened within all the women in the room to live in their full power. I smiled and requested the women place their hands on their vaginal area and breathe into their vaginas.

"Inhale air from the mouth, as though we were drinking with a straw. That same movement of the mouth, do with your vaginas, as though drinking water from the vagina and contracting upwards the circular pelvic muscles of the vagina," I said and I demonstrated with my mouth, sucking in with the noise of drinking with a straw.

"Breathe inwards, from a place of agreeing to a life lived in your own power, into your vaginas. See a pillar of light come through the floor of the pelvis, through the vulva, into the vagina and the uterus. An ever-expanding and shimmering pillar of light."

I asked them to ball their fingers into a fist, so that their hands would help them clench the vagina. They breathed a few breaths like that before I continued speaking: "In breathing this way, the breath fills us with vitality and essentiality. I invite you again to ask your vaginas what it means for them to live a life in full power? What is an empowered vagina or an empowered woman?"

Ember, Iris, Carol, and Ellie closed their eyes and took a deep breath together. Iris opened her eyes wide and said: "An empowered woman agrees to learn all the time; manages to talk about her troubles and she is comfortable with her trials and tribulations. It's hard for me to talk about my own pain, not to mention the subject of sexuality. For most of my life, I couldn't communicate comfortably with my husband. I have much more growing to do around my own empowerment."

"Basically, even identifying that you have more to grow in regards to your empowerment is already standing in your power," I said. "When we identify it, the development has already begun. I invite you to take a deep breath and really say to yourself that you love yourself, even when you don't manage to talk about the pain and difficulties that come up during in a sexual encounter. Be with that place of pain; do not abandon yourself. We have abandoned ourselves too many times. Now is the time to stay and learn to love ourselves as we are. All of you, breathe in that promise to be there for yourselves in love, even when it's hard for you and it hurts. Whisper to yourselves: I am loved, I love myself, even when I don't manage to talk about my pain and my sexuality."

I invited whoever was comfortable to do so to simply to hug themselves and tell themselves that they are loved, even when they don't manage to communicate their pain. Some of the women surrendered easily.

Ruth moved places a few times before resting her hand on her chest and from there, moved her hand down her arms, to her thighs, ending up back with her palms over her heart. Slowly, but surely, the space filled up with the frequency of self-love. A soft and comfortable vibration filled the room, bringing in an energy of simplicity and acceptance.

"I want you to sit opposite one of the other women next to you. One will release and agree to accept love and the other will look into her eyes, with kind, loving, accepting eyes. She will tell her that she loves her—even when it's hard for her to talk about her pain, even when it's hard for her to find the words to talk about her sexuality.

The women sat opposite one another. It seemed that some of them had never sat for a period of time looking straight into the eyes of another person. Saying a prayer to myself, I asked that they be supported. I asked all of them to let go, to relax their shoulders and unwind. I know from experience the difficulties involved in surrendering to a direct gaze of love, into another's eyes for an extended period of time, how very challenging it is to maintain the gaze.

"Those on the receiving side of the love," I said, "breathe a deep breath into the feeling of surrender, giving into what is happening. To those giving the love, I invite you to devote yourselves to unconditional giving. Just give your partner a look from a heart full of love, without using words. With readily kind eyes, the givers of love should want only to give more and more love. Let go, each one of you, into agreeing to give or accept love. Breathe deeply and simply be whole with whatever arises. Breathe, melt into the agreement to give love and to receive love."

The women practiced this for a few minutes. I saw that towards the end of the exercise, even those who found it hard to receive love at first had moments of success and were able to be in the presence of agreeing to receive love.

"Slowly bring the exercise to a close. Great! Please give thanks to one another. You are invited, if you'd like, to give them a hug," I said.

The women hugged each other and even swapped a few words of thanks.

"Thank you," I said. "I want to hear how it was for you all."

"Truthfully," said Ember, "I couldn't begin to describe just how difficult it was to look into the eyes of another person for a long time. In and of itself, that situation was so very intimate and awkward. I never imagined it could be so very challenging."

"Did you give love or did you receive love," asked Iris.

"I gave," said Ember. "It was really fun to give love. It's like bubbling up with champagne to see the happiness in the eyes of Ruth, who sat opposite me. I felt that at the beginning, it was hard for Ruth, but after a few minutes, where her eyes had been darting around, looking in every direction, something changed. She gave into my loving gaze and all her facial features changed. Something softened and became so much gentler and brighter!"

"Honestly, it was really hard, at first," said Ruth, adding: "I felt awkward and sensed that my eyes were evading her, afraid from the intense, penetrating stare inside my eyes, straight into my intimate place. I was alarmed by the unexpected proximity. But then, I decided that I would commit to it, to put my fear to one side and agree to be in the direct line of Ember's eyes. I really felt that I was choosing love. What happened to me during and after was so very pleasant and heartening, I melted. My heart opened and I felt love like I haven't felt in such a very long time! It was a truly transformational experience for me. I understand just how much in my life I avoided opportunities to encounter the world through my heart! Thank you!"

"Imagine what could happen when you agree to meet the world with an open heart and with an empowered vulva! How much new information and experiences you will have in your life!" I said jokingly, knowing all the while that between the lines, I was hinting at the added potential in their life. "Do you think you could describe that moment as one of experiencing your inner power?"

"It was absolutely a moment of choice," said Ruth. "I can define it with the headline of choice from a place of power. Agreeing to surrender to love through conscious choice came from great inner strength. It's easier for me to criticize myself than it is to be in a loving space for a certain period."

"Surely it's obvious that I would choose a life of love, happiness, and inner freedom and I understand how it is connected to my power," said Ellie. "What I don't understand is why people choose otherwise. Of course, it's better to live a life of love."

"You are still young," said Beth. "In life, when there are challenges, unexpressed anger accumulates, grievances with a million different people, and from the hardships of life, sometimes, it is very difficult to simply choose love. Really, life is sometimes very hard."

"That takes us back to the point of choosing love from a place of power, because with all the stresses in life, it is easy to enter into an inner mentality of self-pity and victimhood," I said.

"It's possible to get out of those places and choose a vision of goodness, creating a moment of power and presence in the present. The ability to hold love, for a period of time, in life and during the act of love, is a choice in our power. Do you know that situation when, during love-making, there is a moment of grace where you feel great pleasure and then, exactly at that same moment, you start thinking about supermarket shopping or the errands that you have to do? And just like that, you are not able to be present in the experience of pleasure. You got into your head! The ability to identify, to breathe, and to choose to be present is a choice to be in your power."

"Essentially, what you're saying is that every time I identify that my thoughts are racing and I am not fully present in the moment, whether during sex or not, it's a moment to choose my power?" asked Iris.

"The very fact that you identified that you weren't present," I said, "is already coming back to your power. If you are actively bringing yourself to the present, that's already taking responsibility. When you are in your power you learn skills to take responsibility from A to Z.[8] It is healthy to take responsibility; it makes us better and helps us grow. Being present in your power is to let go of your thoughts and release into the act of love, surrendering to pleasure or to anything that arises from the act of love. You have let go: You are consenting, receiving love, present in your feminine role of the receiver, releasing and surrendering in your fullness to the masculine energy. In moments like these, we are afforded the opportunity to heal. If you are not present, it might be too scary."

"I want to add," said Ember, "I feel an empowered woman is not superwoman or, more accurately, superman... It's not a woman whose masculine energy is the energy that drives her, but actually the opposite: she owns both the masculine and the feminine in her. She knew how to be soft and malleable and knew how to put clear boundaries when needed. That's fruitful cooperation."

"What you are describing is a utopian scenario. How would we even get there?" asked Ruth.

"A part of being in our power is agreeing to live with our

8. The word responsibility in Hebrew is 'achrayut,' which starts with an A, and ends with a T, the last letter in the Hebrew alphabet and signifies responsibility for the full spectrum of life.

weaknesses and to accept them. If I am frustrated, restless, bummed out, my vagina is tense, with an inability to receive penetration, I am not going to belittle or deny these feelings and experiences. On the contrary, I will give them a place and not criticize myself over the fact that I want to make love, but when it comes down to it, I am clenched up and I am blocked." I took a deep breath and continued: "That's power to say we are not able to accommodate or hold this right now. An empowered woman respects the variety of sensations that pass through her, dictates the pace that is right for her, gives place for the tensions, for the stubbornness, for the joy, the pleasure, the tenderness, for everything that she goes through, and practices development through all her experiences."

"And what about if it's for a fuller-figured woman?" asked Beth, pained. "For years, I've been in a love-hate relationship with my body. What about that? According to what you say, an empowered woman loves her body even when it's fat...."

"I recommend that you not ignore the parts of your body that you don't love. When you try to push it away, you are abandoning that part. I invite you to go look in a mirror and tell yourself that you love all of you—yes, also or especially the parts that you criticize."

Beth responded, half laughing and half with ridicule. I heard the protestations in her heart and continued: "An empowered woman loves her body. Every piece of her body is incredible in her eyes, including her folds of fat. How do we do that? We practice more and more, with constant determination, love, and acceptance of all our parts, including the physical appearance of our bodies! Go to the mirror and say to yourself that you are beautiful! Look at each part, see how beautiful you all are! You are all incredible, every one of you! If you look in the mirror and see your ugliness, embrace it—you, the ugliness—because all she usually wants is a hug. When you choose from a place of power, you really do become beautiful, radiant, and sexier. When you are in your power, you become more attractive and people want to be around you to receive your gifts."

Ember shifted uncomfortably and said: "Most of the time, I feel sexy and powerful. But sometimes, without warning, I become two years old. I'm not able to do anything, helpless, and feel like a little girl, really unsexy and powerless."

"Everyone of us has a little girl inside us," I said.

"Girl? I am basically a pensioner!" said Beth, "Any second, you're going to tell me there is a baby inside me, too...."

"It's not nice to say this about myself," said Ruth, "so many people look up to me and ask me for help, but in the face of my separation, I became a little girl and sometimes cried like a baby abandoned by parents who have forgotten she exists and let her cry without picking her up."

"Thank you, Ruth, that is exactly what I meant," I said, explaining: "The little girl that exists inside all of us sometimes becomes the leading cause and influence of our choices in life. Part of life in power is to be able to know these parts that exist within us, to treat those meaningful parts of who we are today with respect. The more we nurture her and deepen our connection, the better it will be for us." I looked at Beth to ensure she understood what I was saying.

"I understand what you mean," said Beth. "I know these places where I am behaving like a helpless child in the face of life. Usually, I just sweep it under the carpet and don't give it a lot of attention."

"When you sweep it under the carpet, there's a high chance the sweet child feels abandoned and hurt. What would support her would be to calm her down with pure love." I looked at the members of the group and felt there was a need to deepen further their connection with their inner child.

"Take a deep breath and call for the sweet, helpless child inside you to come be present. Bring up the parts inside you to conscious awareness and ask her what she wants from you right now, what attention she is asking for."

Beth looked at me as though I were ridiculous. "Seriously, Michal, what are you on about? Do you think I have some kind of split personality?"

"Our bodies hold memories of a little girl who feels uncomfortable in all kinds of situations and sometimes, maybe also feels a little hopeless," I said softly. "Come, try to let go, even if your heads don't fully understand."

I scanned over everyone and looked into their eyes. The room became quiet. The women breathed deeply. Some did not make the transition between the conversation and their introspection as fast as others, but after a few minutes, I felt the women in the room were devoted to creating the connection with their insecure little girl.

"Ask the girl who feels so helpless, what she needs from the adult inside of you?" I asked and gave them a few moments of quiet and introspection. "Now, please say the answers out loud."

The following answers were given: "hug," "a kind word," "more hugs," "love," "a hand of love," "all little girls want loving attention!"

"At the end of the day," I said, "every part of us wants love, even the parts that feel small and weak. A woman who practices living life in her power loves her little and vulnerable girl who lives inside her and is there for her. That little girl also sits in our vagina's memories. She comes up a lot in sexual encounters. When we know how to treat her with respect and in peace, we expand our skills of how to manage our sexual energy and more power and life energy will be available to us," I said.

"And what does it mean when I roam around for months, years, even, in anger over my husband?" asked Iris. "I am not in my power when my anger builds up. From my understanding, it's worthwhile for me to learn to love the short-tempered and angry person I am."

"Correct," I said. "Underestimating our anger, repressing the lack of relating to whatever angers us, creates a volcano that at the end of the day will eventually erupt. Part of the ability to cultivate life in power is to work with our anger, to try not to shout at people we love, but rather to go out into nature to free our anger. For example, go to the forest and scream out our anger. To learn to speak respectfully and to share with whom we are angry with our feeling, to take care of issues that hurt us and not to ignore them. Great tension accumulates around the vagina: anger and frustration that is tied to dissatisfaction, from a touch that was unpleasant for us and we didn't say so, to an ejaculation of sperm inside us that wasn't in time with our ability to contain it and more... If we ignore it, hide it, or don't address it, it will come back to hurt us eventually. Part of life in presence and power is to pay attention to the anger that comes up around our sexuality and to deal with those resentments. Freeing the vagina from anger and frustration that sits inside it is a choice to be in our own power," I said.

"I have attended many workshops on the subject of sexuality," said Ember, "and I understand that the sexual energy is part of the whole energy that constitutes my being. When I learned to work with my sexual energy in my daily life, it's not only in situations with men, but also as part of my whole energy. I will be more in my own power, I will have more energy, I get that. But at the end of the day, I am still very far from that point. I barely know how to work with my sexual energy even in a sexual situation. I have no idea how to integrate that frequency into my daily life, but it's obvious to me that having a clear understanding of it and being present from within is part of my full power."

"It's really sad," said Ruth, "that there is so much sickness, violence, misunderstanding, shame, and fear around the source of the most powerful thing connecting us to our power, to G-d, to the divine spark that comes through us. Every woman who gives birth feels that divinity when she is in labor and that's the power of the vagina. I am a religious woman and G-d is a very important part of my life and yet even so, I didn't register the depth of the absurdity. The place with the utmost connection to G-d is the very place that is indecent and forbidden." Her eyes opened wide and it seemed as though a new passion was burning inside. I was glad to hear her speak up on such things. It was wonderful that such wisdom and knowledge flowed from more women in the workshop.

"That connection to the source, to the divine spark, to creation, is present in our vulva as a collective behavioral pattern," I said, "inside our DNA. The more we choose to empower and free our vulva, the more we allow additional energy of creation to flow in ease in the place that is the closest to G-d, and more from the power of creation of life is able to flow through us." My words were met with silence. The sounds of saturated earth were heard clearly; the streams of water formed in the courtyard from the abundance of rain that had fallen and created a pleasant melody.

"Let's talk about pleasure. What does pleasure have to do with a life of fulfillment and in your full power in the world?"

"Sexuality is not something pleasurable for me," said Beth. "I did it because I felt I had to. Every now and then, I felt a little pleasure, but nothing particularly profound, and now, since my husband passed away, sexuality is not even a part of my life, let alone sexual pleasure. When I try to roll back memories of moments of sexual pleasure, what comes up are dim memories that fill me with a lot of energy, but it was so very long ago," she said as tears choked her throat. "I miss him so much. It's true that we didn't always get along, but I was with him for so very many years and he was a part of me. How could he do this to me? To leave me alone," she wept. "I haven't cried for years," she explained. "This talk of pleasure and power has made me cry. The separation from him pains me."

"Cry, cry, Beth, always after I cry, everything becomes easier for me," said Ellie. Ember got up and brought Beth a tissue to wipe her tears. Beth continued to sob and Ruth went to sit next to her and hug her. Beth began to calm down. Outside, an additional bout of rain fell.

"Thank you for your candor, Beth," I said. "And thank you for your tears. We are here together. You reflect the pain of separation for all of us from people who we love. When we cry, we cleanse our pain and sorrow. Let the water of your tears wash us from inside. Part of being in our power means consenting to expand the range of our feelings; that if we are sad or hurt, we make room for that pain and sadness. That is power! We are not weak when we cry. The opposite! Our tears cleanse us and, afterwards, give us more space for the water of life to flow through us."

"Something is coming up for me now, when you are talking of the water of life, that connects to power and pleasure," said Ember. "Sexual pleasure is connected to fluids. When a woman is aroused and enjoying pleasure, she secretes fluids from her body, not to even talk about female ejaculation, the *amrita*, which can be almost half a cup of water that squirts out of the vagina. Sometimes, too, there can be sweat during love-making— basically, it's a lot of water! Water of love and life. Pleasure brings life and life brings vitality, focus, and courage, the feeling that nothing can throw you off when you are in that space." Ember spoke enthusiastically and all eyes were on her.

Beth raised her head, looked at Ember through her tears, and said: "What half cup of water are you talking about exactly? I don't know whether to laugh or simply keep on crying...."

Iris continued on from Beth's remarks in a fearful, but determined manner: "A woman secretes fluids from her vagina, which is expressed differently throughout her monthly cycle, each time in a different form, I get that, but what are you talking about when you say female ejaculation? I've never heard of that concept in my entire life," she said with her eyebrows raised in amazement.

"I actually have heard of it once from a friend, but I didn't dare ask her for more details," said Carol, and it was clear from her body language that such a topic was not exactly comfortable for her.

"How hidden is the knowledge relating to sexuality," I said. "Only at the age of 42 was I exposed to information about female ejaculation and immediately, I went to study it. Female ejaculation is called Amrita nectar. It refers to the fluid that comes out of the vagina of a woman and sometimes also comes out of the urethra as urine. The fluid arrives in a moment of orgasm, at the peak of pleasure. For years, the medical community couldn't explain it and women almost never talked about it. Now, this knowledge is coming to light more and more. This is a very sacred moment that allows women to connect to more of their power and energy."

"I've never heard of that before," said Ellie. "Even my mother, who did talk to me about sexuality, doesn't know about that." I looked at Ellie and pondered her heart, her innocence, in my heart, thinking of the hardness of life that had not yet touched her.

"Female ejaculation is a conversation for the advanced class," said Carol. "I find it hard just to reach a regular orgasm," she said and took a deep breath. I felt happy hearing her courageous honesty and for the candor of her words.

"I discovered that it's really hard for me to be in pleasure," she continued. "I get to a certain point where I disconnect from my body and random thoughts seize me, so I am left with a kind of flat sexuality, a little pleasurable, but no frenzy of sensations. When I was younger, sometimes, I had stronger orgasms, but with motherhood and the decade that I was married and all the hassles of life, I am less and less able to give in to pleasure. I want more pleasure to be present in my life. It's really hard for me to talk about myself so candidly and moreover on such an intimate subject. Maybe it's the water that is erupting through me," said Carol with a half-smile.

"I am a sexual woman. I love to feel pleasure, but I feel I may die of fear at even the idea of losing control. Truthfully, sometimes, I am so afraid to let go of all my endless thoughts that I can't simply give in to what could be pleasurable!" finished Carol, and it seemed as though, as she spoke, her stature had risen.

"It felt good to hear that," said Iris. "You're motivating me. I am also a sexual woman. I love to indulge, but am afraid to turn into some kind of uncontrollable, wild animal. I am not able to take it anymore. I really suffer from not allowing myself to relax. From a very young age, I was taught to hide and to be ashamed of my sexuality. I can't believe I am about to say this publicly, but I am a sexual being and I consent to relishing in my pleasure and my sexuality!" Iris's voice was confident and brave, mixed with pain. I was moved. I waited for this moment in which magic happens from itself, when women dared to talk and express more of themselves. I felt full with gratitude to G-d and I said in my heart that's exactly what I want more of in the world, more of in the workshop.

"Do you feel how the frequency of power has entered the room? That's what I want to enter into your lives: when you are cooking, when you are tidying your homes, when you make love, when you are driving your car, and so on.... The more you agree to let the pleasure frequency be, the more power will be available to you.

"Pleasure can force us to meet our greatest pain or fears," I said. "Iris said that she may die of fear. When pleasure comes, we are invited to release control, to give into the unknown, and sometimes, that involves the fear of dying."

The moment I paused, Ruth took a breath and asked: "What you're actually saying is for a woman to be in her power, she must choose pleasure as part of her life? That means to see the positive, to bring vivacity to life and to savor that cup of coffee, those strawberries, the sun that caresses my face, the moment when a client comes to me and I succeed in helping her heal her pain."

I looked for a moment at the flames in the fireplace and answered her. "Yes, to allow yourself more pleasure and delight in every aspect of life, including sexual encounters. To agree to pleasure till the tips of your fingers, the end of your nose, and, of course, in your vulva, too. The ability to enjoy yourself, with no connection to other people, is meaningful in the ability to expand and to hold more pleasure in your life. Explore your body, invite yourselves to a sexual encounter with yourselves that releases feelings of guilt and shame. That is power!"

When I mention the subject of self-pleasure to the room, I never know how it will be received. The social taboo creates so much concealment and guilt. I remained silent in anticipation and excitement.

"Come on, stop it, Michal. You keep testing my boundaries!" Beth said once she had calmed down from the many tears that poured out of her eyes. "At my age, you want me to start masturbating? I don't understand how I even got caught up in this workshop. Dear lord, I am in shock! I really remember myself as a little girl and my mother moving my hands away from my vaginal area and telling me doing that is forbidden. Did you experience that, too?" Beth asked everyone and most of the women nodded their heads in agreement. "My mother taught me masturbation is forbidden, not to mention for men, where our religion says spilling the sperm is wasteful. In short, it's forbidden from every angle, for men and for women. Aside from that, I don't even like to touch myself. The few times I tried, it wasn't even nice," said Beth with a half-smile.

The rain stopped. It was almost dark and Beth's words had brought with them the uncertainty, doubt, shame, and fear that revolves around the subject of sexuality. I asked the light forces of the universe to help my words be crystal clear, so they would succeed in landing in the participants' hearts and instigate transformation. Let the participants understand that the release endowed from the meeting of a woman and her body is critical for the ability to live life in power.

I took a deep breath and began to talk: "Your words are important. You have voiced an experience shared by many women. I am not asking you to masturbate. I'm offering you to have an experience where you consciously choose to pleasure yourself.

Certain gates in our bodies will open with a certain touch, unraveling before us pleasure. It might feel weird at the age of 65 to begin to touch your body—I don't know, I still haven't reached that age. I do know in full certainty that the sexual awakening of the body, no matter the age, revitalizes and strengthens our physicality. Pleasurable sexuality is healthy at any age. Inattentive sexuality will constrict, hurt, and be unpleasant for any woman of any age.

"When you develop your sexual touch, you inquire of yourself what feels nice and what doesn't. You feel where there is pleasure and where there is less, which intensity of touch your body requests at any given moment. When you are awake and developing inner listening, you become better at listening to yourself and, in due course, will be able to direct your partner. Our bodies are holy. Physical pleasure is one of the direct gates that connects us to creation and bestows upon us great power and energy. Sometimes, I think religious establishments try to prevent us from tapping into our full power, allowing them to better control people.

"When a man manages to control and direct the life forces that flow through him, to elevate his sperm upwards to his heart and not outwards, he connects to the universal power and raises his frequency. A man's sperm has so much potential for life."

"What does that mean 'when a man elevates his sperm upwards'? I have never heard of such a thing. A man finishes and spills his sperm," said Iris, her eyes widening with a look full of wonder and doubt. I wanted to answer her, but Ember began to talk ahead of me:

"When a man develops his ability to identify the moment before he is about to spill his sperm, he stops, breathes deeply, and squeezes his circular muscles as if he was stopping the flow of urine. The energy rises upwards in the direction of his heart and the sperm doesn't spill out, and that allows new levels of pleasure and hours and hours of love-making."

Beth looked at Ember and, with a smile mixed with wonder, said: "If only that were the case!"

I smiled at Beth and said: "There is always potential. For now, I invite you all to explore self-pleasure. It returns the power to you. You are not dependent on something external to experience pleasure. On the contrary, you choose to merge with a man from a place of abundance, not from a place of lacking."

"That's revolutionary, what is coming up here," said Ellie.

"Life in pleasure is the revolution!" I said with a smile, "Legitimizing sexuality is the revolution!

"I know for sure that when you feel more and more relaxed around the subject of sexuality, the world will be a better and happier place. We have a lot to learn from other cultures that have greater freedom and openness around the lower chakras. I invite you to practice self-pleasure, to relax and empower your vulva, to cleanse and release the patterns around the subject of pleasure, to allow more layers of pleasure within your lives."

"You are giving me so much new information," said Iris, "but can you relate it to the concept of empowering the vulva?"

"An empowered and relaxed vulva is a choice to be in your power. When you are relaxed in your vulva and in every part of your body, when your mind is quiet, you and your partner will be able to devote yourselves to the mystery of love-making and to open to knowledge, wisdom, and love in that sacred time. When your vagina is relaxed, free from contractions, shame, and fear, you will have more energy available to fulfill yourselves.

"I invite you all to practice the skills of listening to the vulva. Listening to the obvious, to the unequivocal, instinctive, vivid, intuitive, and sensory," I said, all the while looking out the window.

"Look at raindrops sparkling in the light of the last sun of the day," I said and everyone turned to look outside as I continued: "See the reflections and all the multitude of colors that are revealed in just one drop! Each one of us has infinite reflections, colors and beauty. Let your beauty sparkle! The sexiest thing is to project your singularity out to the world. When you fence yourselves off and restrict your sexual selves, it is very hard to be attractive and fulfill yourselves."

*I choose to learn to live in my full power, radiating my unique beauty, in serenity and at ease. Thank you, thank you, thank you!!!*

# THE VULVA KNOWS EVERYTHING

I felt it was time to come back to internal observation and to breathing into the vagina, so I said: "Come, ladies, place your hand once again over your vaginal area. We've already talked a lot. Come, we will breathe into her and ask her once more what it means to live life in power."

The women, who had already placed their hands over their vaginal area several times, placed their hands almost naturally and began to breathe into the vagina.

"I want you now to exercise breathing into the vagina in a slightly different way from what we've done so far. Take a deep breath into the opening of the vagina. Feel it, sense it, imagine the inner lips opening so that the air, the energy of life, flows to the edges of the lips and to the anus, which opens and expands as the air enters. Hold your breath for a moment. And now, when you are emptied of air, I invite you to clench your vagina, the circular muscles surrounding it, and as though you are drinking, or, more accurately, from the opening of the vagina, pump the air that is coming from below into yourselves. Come, practice it a few times. Exhale into the vagina, inhale, collect it!"

The women practiced the new breathing technique for a few minutes. "Great, now I ask that you all take in air from the mouth, as you do when drinking from a straw. The same movement happens simultaneously in the vagina as you drink or breathe the life energy from the mouth and the vagina together. The movement is the key for the vaginal canal to move upwards. Remember to breathe and to feel the tickling and stimulation that comes up in the vagina. Keep breathing and give space for that feeling.

"Keep breathing and, at the same time, ask your vulva what it means for her to live in her full power. Answer in the language of the vulva, please!" I said with a big smile on my face.

"Immediately, a request comes up for me to be more connected to my feminine cycles; to my menstruation and my ovulation," said Carol, continuing: "I truly accept that in inner agreement to devote myself to my unique rhythm, so that I will be in my power more and more."

"I hear my vulva, in her unique language, telling me to rest; that my power right now is to consent to find respite," said Iris.

"I feel that my vulva is telling me to free and empower the vulva," said Ember, laughing. "I'm joking, I'm joking... But it's really what my vulva is telling me in her language. What she means is I should let go of the shame to deepen my ability to listen to my gut. I should communicate the sexual being that I am with myself and the world in a crystal-clear manner: through touch, words, and looks; to express my desires, the way I like to be touched; to agree to feel pleasure during sexual encounters with my partner; not to feel stifled or be unable to communicate what is uncomfortable for me, but to feel comfortable enough to share."

"I see a picture of myself breathing," said Ruth. "My vagina is asking that I stop and breathe into her. She is requesting that in my daily life, I stop, breathe, and relax. She is telling me the breath is the key to my power. In those moments where I stop and breathe, greater clarity and inner peace will come to me and become part of me."

"I see a shining, golden light that illuminates my vulva," Ellie said, happily, "like a queen wearing gold jewelry because she knows she is a queen and deserves it. I am a queen and I deserve my kingdom That's what my vulva is telling me: that I am worthy!"

"Wildness—the consent to express the animal inside me, the simplicity around my sexuality," added Ember.

Noa said quietly and confidently: "Acceptance of my

menstruation with joy; presence in my body; to easily say what I feel when it comes to sexual contact."

I added: "To love: to be present with the heart and the love in times of sexual contact."

"Oh boy, even my vagina is talking," said Beth. "Twenty years ago, I would have laughed at the mere idea of it, but here she is, talking to me. My vagina has real words of wisdom. She's telling me she wants freedom."

"I want to add something else," said Carol. "Regarding these infinite fluids that flow in the vagina, my vagina is telling me to love these fluids—the blood, the fertile and infertile secretions. The vagina sits in the pelvis and, as in a basin of water, a constant flow moves through it. Living with these fluids in harmony is part of my power."

"My vulva tells me to stop being disgusted by her, it's enough," said Ruth. "It's about time to stop thinking she is repulsive. She asks that I touch her and treat her and myself with attention and appreciation." Ruth paused and took a deep breath; it was clear that it was hard for her to continue speaking. She took another breath and her eyes filled with tears.

"My power is in loving her and to stop looking with a critical eye at my body, like I need to be some kind of model. I really deserve to feel good about myself and my body," she finished as she leaned back in relief. There was a sense that every additional word she said made her sit more upright and be more present. Ruth finally really feels she is totally worthy. Joy filled my heart and I felt that every one of the women had revealed more of their power. With eyes glowing from happiness, from the renewed powers that I witnessed had been reborn in every one of them, I said: "It has deeply touched my heart that you all came here. We have an all-knowing vulva. When the vulva speaks, she is very clear, sharp, and unambiguous. You are invited, if you wish, to open your eyes."

The women opened their eyes, moved their hand from their vulvas, took a deep breath, and relaxed further.

"When a woman chooses relaxation, life, communication, and love with her vulva, she essentially allows more life, pleasure, happiness, inner tenderness, power, and clarity to be present in her life," I said, and looked at the women to sense the energy in the circle. I felt the quality of deep silence resonate.

Beth took advantage of the quiet and began to speak. "When you speak, it sounds so obvious, but what does it mean to be more of who you are? I am who I am, no?" she asked, partly apologetically, partly in jest.

"Sometimes, my speech is too in the clouds and these questions are great for bringing me back to Earth," I said gratefully. "Our 'self' is infinite in its ability to evolve. The more we develop, the more our cells can contain more of who we are. We expand; more of us can be revealed and create more space in our lives."

I gazed into the fire as the flames were alive and full of movement, and I continued: "When I was 11, I told my mum, a musician, I am not one and quit playing the piano. At the age of 27, a sitar just fell into my hands, and together with it, an unexplainable desire to study, to practice music. With that, I became a musician. At the age of 11, I didn't have a place to express my musical ability, which is why it stopped. Later, more parts of who I am manifested in my body through music."

Beth nodded and smiled in gratitude.

"I understand that inner power and the way that it expresses itself in life are unique to each and every woman," Ember continued the thread of the conversation, "and there is a powerful opportunity to choose each time from anew, because essentially, you could give up music and continue to solidify your belief that you are not a musician, but you chose otherwise. But it escapes me how this is connected to the vulva, relaxing it, or to our empowerment."

"The yoni of every one of us is sacred. It is the gate to creation." I returned to the message. "In the womb, not only our children are created, but also our dreams! With the help of our birth canal, we give birth to our ideas to the world. This understanding gives us power and energy. The yoni is connected to our agreement to birth more of who we are. When you free the contractions of the vagina and you have less physical tension concentrated around your pelvis, it becomes easier to create your unique footprint in the world.

"It's so deep, what you're saying; really important," said Iris excitedly. "I never thought about life like that."

"From this comes the understanding and awareness of our sexual power, which is part of the whole that composes the life force that flows through us! I invite you to pay attention and learn to expand your ability to work with your sexual energy in a conscious fashion when energy is available to support your desired creation. It's part of our power. I will elaborate more on that tomorrow afternoon." The sun had already set and the outside had become dark. I felt the saturation the women were experiencing.

"It's a long-distance marathon run," I said. "Life in power is a life-long lesson! Come, let's take a break for some air, to eat, and to rest.

"We will meet after dinner for a ceremony in which we will connect more to our power—not with words, because speaking about power can bring us insight—but in a ceremony where something happens that is beyond words. We'll go for a break for an hour and a half. Allow yourselves time to rest in your rooms, even a short, dream-filled sleep. Eat well and, if you feel you want a hug, I invite you to feel comfortable to come to me or to any one of the participants, to ask and to accept loving, supportive hugs. We will eat a wonderful dinner in the next room that the chef Rose has prepared for us. She is a dear neighbor and great cook, and we will meet back here at eight in the evening.

All the women left to do their own thing. Some of them went to their rooms in the house next door. Almost all of the women came for dinner, except Beth, who stayed in her room for a good sleep. During dinner, another downpour of rain was accompanied by thunder and lightning. I sat in silence and ate. Ellie sat next to me and asked: "What happened to you at age 20 that at age 42 you began to write a book and create these workshops?"

"Honestly," I answered her, surprised, "I have no idea. I never really stopped to think about it, but I have no doubt that everything is connected. At age 20, I was released from the army. I had no idea what to do, so I flew to be a camp instructor at a summer camp in America. In the army, I was an instructor, too. I had already strengthened my skills in teaching people, from all walks of life, of all shades and ages, and that truly is one of the things I do really well. I simply enjoy doing it. It was a good foundation for what I do now. Do what you love, whatever you feel like doing!"

"I have no idea what I feel like doing," answered Ellie, sadly. "My parents are pressuring me that it's about time I know what I want to do and, truthfully, I simply don't know."

"Don't get bogged down in the 'I don't know,' but instead think this sentence: 'I know that clarity is on its way to me.' Relax, trust yourself from inside, and it will simply come to you." I tried helping the young woman beside me.

"Thanks, Michal. It's good to hear your kind words and see the look on your face that you really trust me. It makes me feel strong," said Ellie.

I looked at her lovingly, then I finished eating and went to rest.

*I choose to love myself, to love the sexual being I am.*
*My femininity is the source of my power.*
*I ask to be supported by the universe to release*
*patterns that no longer serve me and deny me this*
*reality.*
*Thank you for the new knowledge that flows to me.*
*Thank you to the supportive universe.*

# CEREMONY FOR CHOOSING AN EMPOWERED LIFE

I laid down on the bed and sank into a deep sleep. I dreamed a dream in which I crossed through dimensions. I arrived upon a grand temple flooded with golden light; around it, three men were standing, partially guarding it, but also part jailers. I stood, radiant and glowing, as there were visible black and yellow lights inside me, a little like the storm of thunder and lightning outside. I felt the lighting strike and illuminate me, shaking and rattling my very existence. Now, it became clear the three men were sent to guard me during the initiation that was coming to me in this dream. I felt electricity running through me, burning me with fear. My guardians stood confidently by my side, their presence assuring me that I could overcome this fear and emerge from the storm with greater power and electricity. I breathed in deeply, all the while still asleep, but regardless, my breath became faster and faster. The fear had punctured my body and my head was about to explode.

In the background, I heard a woman's soft, familiar voice: "Love; just consent; lower the power that you feel down to your heart. It is your power. You have tremendous ability. You can move through worlds. Breathe; you can do this. Breathe deeper into your womb. You can do this."

During the dream, I breathed more deeply and suddenly, opened my eyes in panic. I understood that the dream was tied to the upcoming ceremony I was planning to hold tonight and that I had just being initiated so I could contain more power. I got up and prepared myself a cup of tea; and put background music of my sister playing in her full charisma and exhilarating power. Her voice helped me relax from the dream and come back to myself. Once again, I closed my eyes and prayed that the ceremony benefit the women in the workshop. I prayed there would be a good connection between the women and myself, and with Natalie, who would come to hold the ceremony with me.

For me, a ceremony is always a leap into the unknown. Usually, I have an idea how I will start a ceremony, but I never know what will happen during it or how it's going to end. Rituals open an opportunity for profound transformation. It's impossible to know when the magic will arrive. It really depends on the ceremony's inherent wisdom and the wisdom of the participants.

I heard Natalie come into the yurt and I left the room to greet her. In one hand, she held a bag full of crystals and in the other a full basket of logs. She put down her belongings and we hugged in an all-enveloping and loving embrace. I prepared a cup of tea for her and together, we went to arrange the space for the ceremony. In the center of the circle, we placed stones, seeds, candles, flowers, and crystals and a crystal bowl full of water. After that, we sat opposite each other, looked deep into each other's eyes, and positioned ourselves for the coming ceremony to ensure there would be clear communication between us; support for the ceremony; and that the energetic physical tool we were preparing for the ceremony would be able to contain the power.

We prayed for supervision, from the virtuous and loving angels, to support us through the ritual, that the ceremony's intrinsic wisdom would be communicated through us clearly and unambiguously. We called upon ancient wisdom of the feminine network and requested support in the space where the ceremony would be held. The energy that flowed was powerful. I was quiet. I knew in my heart of hearts, without a shadow of a doubt, that it was going to be an incredible and meaningful ceremony for all the participants.

The women reassembled in the room. I received them with a smile and a warm hug. The women hugged each other warmly and sat down in the circle.

I brought Natalie in and was reminded of all the journeys we had gone through together. Natalie is a good friend and a sister for the journey. Together, we have gone through the path of discovery of our own power in relation to sexual energy and the ability to bring it into our daily lives. Natalie had a pleasant demeanor and even though she had joined the workshop for the ceremony alone, her presence there was natural. We sat in silence and I started to sing and play on the crystal and Tibetan singing bowls. The sound was pleasant, moving, and relaxing as Natalie held the steady beat of the drum.

"This is Natalie," I said, "I invited her to join me in leading this ceremony and to my great honor, she agreed. In ancient times, a ceremony would be held by the entire community or by a few people together. The togetherness raises and elevates the frequency."

With a big smile and loving look, I gazed into Natalie's eyes and continued: "Natalie, you and I will lift the frequency. We will be a container for the magic that seeks to come through us, to us, especially for us, today!"

I asked the women to breathe deeply into their vaginas and be attentive and observant deep inside themselves. Alongside the drizzle of the rain, we heard the murmur of the women breathing. When the air meets with the body and enters us, a quiet sound is formed, and when we are talking about a whole group of women breathing deeply, the sound has a strong presence.

"Pay attention to the feelings that come up in the vagina. I am turning our attention to the vagina because I want to implement this habit into our daily lives. Start with at least once a day until we get to a place where that discourse and attention are as present and natural in your day-to-day lives as brushing your teeth."

The skies filled with clouds, the moonlight barely poking through. More rainstorms were set to come. A deep and quiet breathing space fell over the room, and it held a shared and harmonious rhythm between the women.

"A ritual is a wonderful opportunity for transformation," said Natalie as she sat next to me. "We invite you to be part of the creation and the active work of the ceremony.

"We invite the wild woman residing in all of you to be present here, along with the quiet woman, the wise, the devoted, and the self-attentive woman," she continued. "We invite the powerful woman to come to us and be expressed in her full presence, gently, sensitively, wildly, in whatever form comes."

"Continue to breathe deeply as we elaborate," I said to continue Natalie's words, "and if you feel the urge to sigh, allow that to come. Now, together, let's take in air and empty it together. Ahhhhhhh..."

Ember released a sigh and then Ellie, Ruth, Noa, Iris, Carol and, in the end, even Beth let out a big sigh.

"Your freeing sighs make me so happy," I said, smiling. "These sighs cleanse, purify, and release us."

"We are starting the phase of purification and release of excess energy," Natalie followed after me. "We will light a sage stick, all the while releasing sighs and nurturing the body. After that, we move on to summoning the components that will support the ceremony. You can call on the directions of the skies, the four mothers from the Bible, or the four elements. Summoning the elements allows us to enter into the ceremonial space with more support, so that the ceremony's magic and the transformation it allows will flow easily and powerfully. We enter the ceremony in one state and leave it in another. We are not able to control the way in which the magic comes. We can choose what inspiration we bring into the space. Each one of us attending the ceremony is present with her own unique connection to the source and is in possession of her own special way in which it will flash through her. I love to call to the seven directions—East, South, West, North, up, down, and to the core. In the next stage of the ceremony, we voice our intentions aloud and pledge inner consent to surrender to the ceremony. Gradually, we will ascend to the climax of the ritual, to allow the materialization of the spiritual energy of the ceremony into matter—that is, we will take concrete action that illustrates the transformation to which we are aiming."

"In this ritual," I continued, "today, we are here together by choice and with the intention of living in fullness and in our full presence in our bodies, including in our sexuality. It's a part of the whole that we are!

"We invite each one of you to bring her uniqueness into the space. We are in a shared process where we support each other to increase the ability to live our life in presence and in power. In projecting our individuality on Earth, we awaken inspiration in those around us to choose to live in their power. I invite you to dedicate yourselves to the grace of the ceremony's frequency. The more you let go of your thoughts and simply surrender to the process, the more your potential to transform will increase.

"I am guessing for some of you, or maybe most of you, this is the first time you will have been in such a ceremony," continued Natalie. "When we act in a different way from the way we are used to, there's potential for a different outcome. We want to achieve a result where each one of us is more in her power, more present. May we have a pleasant flight!" she concluded, smiling, and everyone smiled back at her.

"I want to talk for a moment about fear," I said. "Who is afraid of their own power? Do you know that feeling where you are simply afraid of being seen in the full light of your power? In your stunning beauty?" I asked and immediately continued: "For many of us, it's scary to choose to live in power—to consent to hold all of those parts of us and to give them all space! I know it from my own physical experience of having great power that is stuck in my head and simply scares me. I only relax when I agree to lower the power from my head to my heart and body, and my power can find its natural fulfillment in my daily life. Every few years, I am initiated to more of my power and, at the end of every transition, I experience the fear of death. What is this story all about? Why are we afraid to die? Why are we afraid to burn, to be burned, to perish? What is happening here?"

"On a collective level, we carry memories with us as women, when we were murdered and killed because we lived in our power," said Natalie. "Throughout history, thousands and maybe millions of women who were shamans, healers, doulas, midwives, and sexual priestesses were murdered. They were women who provided services to the community in which they lived. World leadership became male dominated and it became dangerous for women to live in their power. Women whistled on other women and the sorority of sisterhood fell apart. Women stopped congregating together. They stopped summoning, casting spells, dreaming, and spilling menstrual blood together. A number of studies show something in the brain changes in a woman when she meets other women. It does us good! Sisterhood is so very important. When our vulvas feel and know that she is among other vulvas who love and respect her, she lets go of herself and rests! The memory of that injury to the sisterhood and the genuine danger that women who are visibly in their power has stayed in our collective memories and is encoded in our DNA."

The room was quiet, a silence of vibrating agreement, in recognition of the deep pain of the loss of the sisterhood. The great fear of being visible in the world generates a pulsating feeling of anger and an inner question sits inside every woman present in the room: what are we going to do with the fear of living in our power? How can we change the fear so that it will stop dominating us? It was as though we were a droplet, sitting and resting on a leaf until the moment comes when it must fall to the ground.

The drop shatters and its fragments scatter everywhere, forgetting that it was once one whole, large drop. So, too, the women forgot their sisterhood.

"What am I supposed to do now with all that shocking information you have given us? Natalie, my body hurts from what you just told us here...." said Ellie.

"To cleanse ourselves in every way possible from that story that we women and, really, our men, too, have carried inside us for generations," answered Ember.

"I have no idea what you're talking about," said Beth in anguish. "What does it mean to cleanse it?"

"In Judaism, there are many ways to cleanse," said Ruth. "Deep prayer from the heart; plunging into the *mikveh*, [9] a spring, or in the sea. We have a special prayer for breaking vows. There are ways to cleanse, but the most important thing is to hold the belief that liberation and cleansing is possible in the first place."

"Thank you, beloveds, for this important conversation," I said, took a deep breath and kept on: "Let us finish here. A ritual space seeks quiet and devotion. Even if you don't understand something, that's alright. You may ask and, better yet, simply surrender and let the magic of the ritual take you. The moment has come for us to clear our memories and to allow space for our power to flow through us." In a precise voice of intention, enchantment, and exhilaration, Natalie and I said in unison: "Here we go! Ceremony! Ceremony! Ceremony!"

Within a few minutes, all of us stood and, under my guidance, began to drum on our bodies, releasing our voices and sighs with the intention of releasing all that was extraneous and unnecessary. Very quickly, the energy began to build up and the electricity started to be palpable.

Natalie lit a sage stick and passed it, one by one, over the participants, purifying them with the smoke. She focused around the heart, the hips, and under the armpits. The act looked a little different for each of the women. I started to hum "mmm...." I invited the participants to join me. The room was filled with

---

9. A ritual bath.

smoke and a strong smell of sage. The humming sound merged with the drops of rain and the fire in the fireplace looked as though it were dancing to their sounds.

Natalie finished purifying the women and started to thump the grounding heartbeat on the drum—a uniform rhythm that connects the natural heartbeat of the human heart to the Earth. The drumbeat echoed into every cell of everyone in the room.

"Come together, beloved women, let us unite into a unified, holy and loving space," I began to speak the words that came to my mind.

"To create the space that incorporates the support of the entire universe to increase our ability to live in presence, power, and fulfillment! I invite you all to stand facing East. Let's raise our hands together. With a blessed, open heart, we invoke the spirit of the East."

"Come, come to us, spirit of the East," said Natalie. "Support our ceremony. Bring us new winds of new dawns. With the clear knowledge that every day allows us to be reborn and let our uniqueness shine bright. Give us the strength to be reborn into full presence in the body. Welcome, spirit of the East!"

"Come let us say together: welcome, spirit of the East," I said, and the women devoted themselves to respond to the blessed call. I took the matches and lit the candle that faced East, with the intention that the flame bring with it the genuine winds of change and renewal to everyone present in the room and the world as a whole. I sensed that Ruth was embarrassed. Ember surrendered herself to the moment and welcomed the spirit of the East, while the other women joined in and settled comfortably into the unfamiliar state of the ceremony.

I looked towards the fireplace and I exclaimed: "I invite you all to turn a quarter turn to the right and face South. Let us raise our hands together and with heartfelt intent and blessings, we will continue and invoke the spirit of the South.

"Welcome, wind of the South. You are welcome to the

ceremonial space to warm our hearts and to light the fire of life, so the joy of life may reverberate and desire may be awakened. Imagine there are stones around the fire of life that guard and prevent it from spreading everywhere. We invite a balanced, living fire, heated exactly to the right degree, to inspire our sexuality to come to a life in a way that benefits us and gives more vivacity to our souls! Welcome, spirit of the South!"

With the beat of the drum in the background and the flames in the fireplace flickering, somehow intensifying and illuminating even more of the room, the women answered in unison: "Welcome, spirit of the South!"

I handed the matches to Beth to light the candle in the center of the circle that signified the South. She crouched down and muttered to herself, "I've never done anything like this in my life. But here we go, something different from my usual...." Half embarrassed, half smiling, partly pleased with herself, she lit the candle and returned to her place. The voices sounded more secure, more present. The smoke was still billowing from the sage stick that was resting in the center of the circle, between the crystals. Carol was staring at the ashes that fell from the sage. It seemed to me she was troubled by the ash that was about to fall and dirty the white tablecloth.

All the while, Natalie continued to beat on the drum and say: "Take a quarter turn to the right, facing the West. Raise your hands and with an open and blessed heart, invite the spirit of the West. Welcome, spirit of the West, the direction that signifies the element of water." The rhythm of the drum transformed and intensified, and as is the case in many ceremonies, we felt the response of the forces of the universe immediately. It rained harder and drops of water rained down together especially loud.

"The water is responding to us!" I exclaimed happily. "Water, water, cleanse us, lend us support to release and cleanse patterns of holding on to the old, reductive patterns of the feminine towards the masculine, the reductive patterns of the masculine towards the feminine, patterns of hatred and distrust. Spirit of the West, lead us like water that seeps deeply into the belly of Mother Earth, crossing rocks and finding new paths in the depths of the ground, cleansing, purifying, and refining our being. Thank you! Welcome, spirit of the West!"

At the same time, everyone responded: "Welcome, spirit of the West." I ventured into the center of the circle and gently sprinkled water on everyone present. Spontaneously, almost all the women burst forth together in song:

> *"Joyfully draw water,*
> *From the well of bliss,*
> *Water, water, water!*
> *Joyful, blessed water!*
> *Hey, hey, hey...."*

The song continued for a few minutes and filled the space with much joy and triumph.

Natalie then passed the matches to Ruth and she lit the candle of the West. A sacred atmosphere overtook us and sincere and true prayers were said as the candle came to light. It was reminiscent of lighting candles on the Jewish Sabbath. The singing calmed down and the women turned a quarter to the right, to face the North. The drum beat slowed, with long, fixed intervals between the beats.

"Welcome to our ceremonial space, spirit of the Earth," I said. "Earth bears wisdom that has carried such knowledge for generations. We invite the wisdom of the grandmothers, the wisdom of the high mountains, of the northern wind where the mysteries of darkness reside, and the crystals that hold the knowledge of the universe to our space. The cooling spirit that balances and chills the spirits, welcome, spirit of the North!" The drum changed its beat once again, quickening as all the women chanted: "Welcome, spirit of the North!"

I turned back to the center of the circle and with me, the women turned, too. I raised my hands to the sky and the women followed after me as I said: "Welcome, spirit of the above. Wisdom of the father, bring light down to Earth, inspire us from a bird's eye view, allow the clouds to move and the bright spaces to be present in the ceremonial space. Give us the agility of the bird, the infinite light that is available to us according to our inner wisdom. Welcome, spirit of the above!"

I let Ellie light the candle; she was happy and excited. Before she lit it, she closed her eyes, muttered quietly words of prayer, and finally lit the candle. I felt she was going through something deep. I sat down on the ground, resting my hands on the earth and for a moment, I fully bent down and rested my forehead on the ground. Everyone imitated my movement. I took a deep breath, as did everyone else, all together.

"Welcome to our ceremonial space, spirit of below," we said together, "we invite to our ceremony the wisdom of the goddess that resides in the Earth. Caves of your enveloping womb, the water springs that are derived from within you. The healing stones, minerals that build up our body, endlessly nourishing our needs and with the ability to shake and to dismantle systems. Please support us in dismantling and rebuilding the systems. May compassionate blessings of the mysterious Earth that resides within you become visible. Welcome to the ritual, spirit of the below. It is safe for you to be present with us."

"Welcome, spirit of the below," everyone answered. I asked Carol to light the candle. She knelt and lit the candle calmly, yet joyfully. I put my hands in front of my chest in namaste, with the palms touching each other. Everyone did as I did and I said:

"Feel the touch of your right hand against your left. Right meets with left in unity. The encounter between them awakens and reminds us of our center, which lies in the middle of our bodies and can, according to our inner wisdom, extend far beyond. Collect and release the circular muscles of the vagina and anus, as this area also reminds us of the center of the body. In each one of us, we call to presence the core of the ritual. Come to us! In radiant presence, of knowledge, bright and simple and all-knowing, welcome, spirit of the center.

"Welcome, spirit of the center," everyone responded. Natalie asked Ember to light the central candle that was inside the crystal bowl filled with water. I asked everyone to take a breath and release the "ah" sound.... A sighing "ah...." was audible. The women were dressed in a wide variety of colors and with the release of the sign, I was sure the colors shone even brighter in the dimly lit space.

"Let us breathe even more together," said Natalie. "While breathing, place your left hand on your own heart and your right hand on the back of the heart of the woman on your right. Put your hand slightly above the center of your heart, towards her upper back. We'll breathe together into the heart, creating a circle together, heart to heart. The hands are extensions of our heart. With our left hand, we will accept love and with the right, we will give love to the woman next to you."

I sat in the center and played the crystal bowls. The sound that passed through the room was high, tremulous, and penetrating. From experience, one can feel the sound move from the body and flow intermittently between the right and left sides of the body and enter deep inside. An atmosphere of deep unity was created between every woman. After a few minutes, once the energy had built up, I said:

"Great. Keep breathing. Take a deep breath into the heart and each one of us will say to herself: 'I agree, I accept,' and on exhale: 'I consent, I give.'"

After a few moments of shared, quiet, and full breathing, I kept on speaking: "Notice the sensations passing through you. How many worlds can open for us when we agree to receive and consent to giving? Energy flows more freely and with more simplicity and allows the flow of life to simply be. Come, let us remember;

remember and be with the intention of today's ceremony. You are invited to say after me aloud. Smile and place the frequency of joy, confidence, and determination into the intention: 'I choose....' Everyone said after me, in eloquent and brave voices, "I live life being present in my body and in my full power!" The women repeated after me. I stomped my feet on the ground and everyone stomped after me rhythmically, like a beat of a drum, creating a unified and powerful network. The energy in the room rose. Natalie continued drumming to the beat of the stamping and after a few more minutes, slowly, we slowed the tempo, finally stopping. There was total silence mixed with exciting intensity.

I felt an energy of deep gratitude inside me and told the women: "Rest your hands on your heart. Let us say thanks for what we have, even for the fear. We are grateful for the fear of death that is present in our bodies; grateful for the added layer ]we needed to hide our power; grateful for the hatred towards men; for the need to control the man who was next to us or the need to belittle ourselves; for the inability to express ourselves comfortably; for the fear to say no when no was what was right for us; for agreeing to be penetrated when we didn't want to be; for the times we froze. Thank you. Thank you. Thank you for it being difficult to say thank you. I invite you to be in true and simple gratitude, out of respect to every feeling that may arise, even anger, insult, or injury. Take a deep breath and continue to be grateful!"

I stood up next to Beth. I saw her face scrunch up; her shoulders were shrugged tight to her face. From her body language, I detected she was going through a tough time and needed a supportive presence beside her. I looked at her with gratitude and continued to talk.

"Thank you for the sexual woman I am. Thank you for my sexual handicaps. Thank you for not being able to admit to the world that I am a sexual being. Thank you to the extremely sexual being, who only ever comes out in private and to the sexual being who hides herself all her life. Thank you to the woman who has no

131

idea how to deal with their sexual energy. Thank you to the wise woman who knows how to handle her sexual energy. Thank you, thank you, thank you!"

"You know," continued Natalie, "sometimes, we blame ourselves for the sexual woman inside of us. She shows up and we become filled with guilt. Come, let us say thanks to that feeling. Bring up the guilt now; give it a place; thank the feeling for being present in your life. There was a moment when that guilt had a meaningful role in taking care of you."

"Taking care?" asked Beth and Ruth simultaneously, but Natalie carried on: "Yes, taking care of you, protecting you. The guilt saved us from harm, from a situation where our sexuality was not appropriate. It is no longer relevant and it is possible to simply thank it for the service it has provided for us in our lives, throughout entire incarnations."

"And what about the shame that eats me up inside just for being sexual? Should I thank the shame, too?" asked Ember.

"Thank you for bringing up shame," I said and began to sing:

*"Shame, shame,*
*How very afraid I was of shame,*
*How shrunken,*
*How very degrading you are. It's a sham, shame,*
*Sham, shame,*
*How much I was ashamed,*
*Yes... yes...*
*I was ashamed...*
*Shout out to shame, dear girls,*
*Look at her in the eyes and tell her that you love her,*
*Thank her for the service she provided you,*
*Yes, dear shame,*
*With great shame."*

I continued, half smiling, "With great power and great presence, I thank you. I love you. I am thankful to you for what you did to keep me safe. You put a full chastity belt around my pelvis, my vulva, my vagina, my anus, and my buttocks. Thank you, shame. Thank you for the chastity belt. I love you for the dedicated service you have provided me.

"Enough abandonment of ourselves," I continued. "I invite us to agree to simply hold everything that is, in love and lightness. Even if difficulties come up, those are just fine," I said as I kept eye contact with Natalie, who was playing the crystal bowls and then lit the sage stick.

We both felt how hard it was to thank guilt and shame, feelings that create so much blockage and anxiety within us all. We breathed together and tuned into the frequency of gratitude to whatever exists, without criticism. Gratitude from our heart of hearts, which creates more room for thanksgiving, love, and recognition of the goodness that exists and is present in our lives.

"Let's pair up," Natalie suggested. "Look each other in the eye and ask for forgiveness. Michal and I will demonstrate," she said when she noted the confusion in everyone's eyes. I stood up in front of Natalie, we looked each other in the eye, and immediately, tears began to pour out from me.

Natalie began to speak: "I ask for forgiveness from myself, from the creator inside of me, for being ashamed of being sexual. I ask forgiveness for being afraid to be present in my body."

"I forgive you, I forgive you, I forgive you," I answered her, as my eyes were moist from tears. I looked deep into her eyes.

"Open your eyes and gaze at the person in front of you with compassion, even if it is difficult," Natalie requested and then turned back to me: "I ask forgiveness for being ashamed of the sexual being I am." Natalie waited and the women repeated after her, some of them quietly and others in a louder voice.

"I ask forgiveness for not trusting the sexual being I am,"

said Natalie. The women repeated after her as others, who were listening, observed compassion and love.

"I ask forgiveness for criticizing the sexual being I am," said Natalie, as everyone repeated her words. As Beth said the sentence, she looked as if she had shed some of the wrinkles on her face and was standing more upright.

"I ask forgiveness for not having the courage to be who I am and stand in my full power," said Natalie.

"I forgive you." The statements were heard one by one.

We had dimmed the lights. Many candles were lit in the space. I felt the frequency rise, the fire illuminating the room. I observed the women, eyes closed, dedicated to the intent to forgive. I returned to beat the drum and Natalie said: "I ask forgiveness for the disconnection from my body. I ask forgiveness that I am afraid to be visible in the world with my sexual power."

The women repeated after her like an echo. The sentence was heard again and again throughout the space: "I ask forgiveness for being afraid to be seen by the world with my sexual power."

I increased the rhythm of the drum and Natalie raised her voice, saying again: "I ask forgiveness for being afraid to be seen by the world with my sexual power." The echo got louder and resounded in the room.

As I was playing the drum, a small smile danced across my face. I let my hair loose and I felt the presence of my inner wild being take me into the ecstasy of ceremony. I devoted myself to the wisdom of the ceremony coming through me. I moved confidently among the women, strengthening them with my gaze and presence; and encouraging them to dare to break out of their shells, to free their inner wild woman, the woman that doesn't think ten times before she dares to appear.

"I forgive myself for making myself small and reducing myself by men," I said and the women repeated after me.

"I forgive myself for making myself small and reducing myself by men," I returned and said, my eyes filled with tears. The women were emotional and tearful, too.

"It hurts to look with eyes open, but many of us have reduced ourselves in the face of the masculine within us and outside of us in our relationships with men. Let's face this pattern and forgive ourselves for that presence. It's a pattern that women have carried within themselves for generations upon generations. Come, let us break the chain, free our girls from that karma, and allow ourselves to be present in who we are, without the need to be small or to belittle any man who stands beside us."

I said the sentence again and asked the women to say it with me. This time, with a more forgiving tone, softly, and trusting that something new would be able to be born from inside. The phrase "I forgive" sounded clearly again and again, as though each apology was chasing after another. Compassion was felt in the air and allowed forgiveness to reverberate even deeper.

Beth cried out in full devotion: "I forgive myself for making myself small for men. How small I was, oh my!" Why did I do that to myself? And for so very many years? Even after my husband, G-d bless his soul, passed away, I continued to belittle myself. Oh...my, how small I made myself. I was so small, like a fingernail. Who even am I? Who will I become? I don't even know who I am? What should I do? I am not prepared to make myself small again for a man. I wish, Amen, that G-d allows me to correct this," she continued to cry out.

All the women stopped, dumbstruck. Natalie and I moved closer to her, respecting the intimate space between her and Ember. As I played the drum, I asked: "Are you ready to be great?"

Beth looked at me with desperation, as though she didn't know how to answer me, and she burst into tears, mumbling: "I don't know, I don't know, I don't know how.... I don't know what it means to be great."

The drum continued to play as Ember wrapped her in her arms and whispered to Beth in her ear: "I forgive you, I forgive you, I forgive, forgive, forgive."

"You forgive me?" Beth asked in wonder.

"I forgive you and do you forgive me?" Ember asked. Beth took a deep breath, as all the women stood in a circle around her, feeling that what had come from Beth with so much power lives within each one of them in such a personal way.

I prayed for her good health and asked for more support and courage for her to endure what she was feeling.

Natalie moved closer to Beth and rested her hand on Beth's upper back, behind her heart. I started to chant words that sounded as if they were from an ancient Native American ritual:

"Ana, whe, whe, hey, Ana whe whe hey, Ana Na O Ana Na Hana, Ana wow na Hana hey, Ana na Ana na, hey, hey hey hey hey," my voice grew louder. I repeated the sentence again and again. Ember enveloped Beth in her embrace.

Beth started to mumble: "I am afraid, I am afraid, so very afraid. I don't know what to do. I don't even know how to be great. How can I be great? I have been small for so very many years. What, now I will suddenly become great? How do I even do that?"

"Do you want to be great?" asked Natalie, her hand still on Beth's back.

"Of course, I want that," said Beth, "but the truth is I am deathly afraid."

"Great. Be with the fear," answered Natalie. As though possessed with madness, Beth shouted: "What do you mean 'great'? I'm telling you I am about to die!"

I went to the side of the room to bring a mattress from the stack. I put it down and asked Beth to lay on top. Beth laid down on her stomach, her face to the ground. Ember sat by her and rested her hand on Beth's back and the other stroked her hair. Beth was sobbing, all the while continuing to insist: "I am dying, I am dying."

Once again, I picked up the drum and drummed the beat around her body. The women sat in a circle around her and began to rest their hands upon her. Ruth began to whisper, murmuring and pledging the Jewish prayer "Hear, O Israel."

Soft, compassionate, feminine song, and deep adherence to the Creator was heard and began to resonate in the space: "Hear, O Israel: the LORD is our God, the LORD is one." The song grew stronger and Beth cried more and more. Iris sat by Beth's feet, with a look of love and compassion. I felt inside her desire to put her hands on Beth's feet. She placed them there and then took them off again. I realized she had to overcome the fact that Beth couldn't give her permission to do so. From afar, I sent her supportive energy for the courage to listen to the call of her heart. Iris put her hands upon Beth's ankles, as, at the same time both Ellie and Carol placed their hands upon Beth, Ellie on her stomach and Carol on her feet. I kept playing the drum. Natalie removed her hand from Beth's back to light a stick of Palo Santo, a small piece of wood that releases smoke that purifies the space, fosters the exchange of energy, transforms negative energy, soothes, and opens the airways.

Iris inhaled the unfamiliar scent, which immediately gave her confidence that her choice to place her hands upon Beth was correct. Beth calmed down. She succumbed to the loving touch of the women and gave a sigh now and again. Natalie finished purifying the space and put her hand back on Beth's back.

"I am still terrified," she said. "Now, I am a little more relaxed. I don't entirely know what it means to be great. My whole life, I made myself small...." she said and began to cry again.

"I also make myself small," said Iris. "You are not alone."

"Even at work at the hospital, I belittle myself," said Ruth.

I looked around and saw that all of the participants were identifying with each other, recalling that feeling and experience when one had given up her power to someone else and afterwards felt small.

"You are definitely not alone," I said. "We are here with

you, crossing this gate of agreement to live life in our full power, together." I looked Beth in the eye and kept talking to her and to all those present: "We are with you. You are not alone. You are not alone. I agree and live in full presence and power. I agree. I agree to live in full presence and power," I said again with the beat of the drum.

Beth joined me and said: "I agree. I agree. I live in full presence and in my full power. I agree. I agree. I am a sexual being, yes, yes, yes. I agree. I agree, I walk with confidence on the Earth," she began to sing.

Ember, whose hands were still resting on Beth, joined her, followed by Iris and Ellie.

"I agree, I agree,
Yes, I am fully present,
Yes, I am sexual and so I am!
Yes, I am sexual and so I am!
I am sexual ya, ya, ya.
I am walking in confidence on the Earth,
I am walking in confidence on the Earth,
In serenity, yes, yes, yes,
In serenity, I agree."

I joined the singing in a melody that emerged from me as I kept up the beat of the drum in the background.

"In serenity," sang Ember out loud, as Beth joined her: "In serenity, yes, ya, G-d, I am deathly afraid, so show me how to be in serenity...."

Natalie and I sang in synchronicity and harmony, in a clear, powerful voice: "I agree, I agree to walk with confidence in my sexual power. I am sexual!" I increased the volume and power of the drumbeat with the song as it got louder and louder.

"I agree," sang Beth.

"I recognize and appreciate the sexual being that I am," Ember sang.

"Yes, yes, I am sexual, even though I hid it very, very well!" Carol added.

"I am great," Ellie said as everyone joined in the beat of the trance, singing together: "I am great. I am sexual and great." Beth laid down on the mattress and murmured to herself: "I can't believe I'm in such a weird situation."

Only those close to Beth heard what she said. Ember retorted: "Believe it. Believe, give into it. You are receiving a gift here."

"I am about to faint, whatever is happening here is so powerful," she wailed. "I feel like I'm about to die," she told Ember breathlessly.

I moved closer to her and said: "It's ok to be afraid to die. Allow whatever wants to die simply to die. Take a deep breath, my love." I saw that Iris had deepened her grip on Beth's ankles.

Beth said: "It feels good that you are touching me; it relaxes me. Honestly, no one has ever touched me like this. It's helping me to cross the fear. Carry on."

Ember put a hand on Beth's heart from behind and added: "Simply give in. We are here for you, for us all."

We stood around her, very close, singing together in a voice that grew stronger: "I agree, I am a sexual woman! I am happy. I am a sexual woman." Something from the power and intense energy present in the room began to touch Beth. From her Beth's voice ,it was clear that it overcame her and broke through; and she found herself singing together with the other women:

"I agree. I am great. I am sexual!"

As Beth's voice merged with the rest of the women, a deep agreement descended on the room, entering deep inside each and every cell of the participants.

I stood up. Ember gave Beth her hand and helped her to stand, too. We stood together, close to each other. A tribe of women, sisters to the journey, who support each other along the way.

The drum played and everyone together continued to sing at the top of their lungs: "I agree. I am great. I am sexual. I am happy. I am a sexual woman. I am great. I am sexual. I agree. I am great. I am sexual. I am sexual." Everyone moved, stamping their feet and singing loudly. All at once, I gave the final beat of the drum and the room was filled with complete silence.

"Repeat after me," I requested. "Here and now, I am relinquishing the vows I made in all periods of my life, in all worlds, times, dimensions, and levels."

Everyone repeated after me in one unified voice. In my head, I heard Ruth's thoughts and I said: "In Judaism, it is customary to relinquish vows in a *minyan*[10]. We are not ten men, but we are an incredible group of women who have chosen to be in our power and presence and agree to witness ]this defining moment, agreed?" I asked and everyone, in a chorus, answered: "Yes."

"When something is done in public," began Natalie, "when there are other witnesses to an action or statement, it has been given the seal of approval to be upheld and fulfilled. All of us have sanctioned these vows and have been witnesses to these vows being taken at the same time."

"Let us say it again," I requested. "Here and now. I am relinquishing the vows that I made in all periods of my life, in all worlds, times, dimensions, and levels." The women repeated after me decisively.

"I release the vows that prevented me from living a life in balance between the masculine and the feminine within myself and within my relationships," I said, "the oath that prevented me from being in full presence in my body and living life in my power. I choose life!" The women repeated my words in a powerful presence and I continued: "Here and now, I choose and reclaim the right to live in presence and full power." The echo of the women returned to me loud and clear.

I took a deep breath and continued when I felt the energy of the room get more and more powerful: "I choose a life in balance

_____

10. A quorum of ten Jewish men required for certain religious obligations.

and honor between the masculine and feminine within me, in renewed partnership between male and female." The women repeated after me word for word. "We choose courage, together with fear of death," I said and the women echoed the words.

Natalie brought the straw basket full of wood logs and every one took a log for themselves.

"We will put the logs in the fire," said Natalie, "with an intention of releasing the pattern of fear of getting burned; releasing the pattern of making ourselves small in the face of the masculine energy; releasing the pattern of trying to control the masculine energy; releasing the pattern of fear from the masculine energy; releasing the patterns of victimhood; and releasing the victimized vagina."

"Let us give thanks for these patterns we carried with us for generation upon generation," I said as I held a chunk of wood in one hand. "We will put our left hand on the center of our hearts and say: 'in gratitude, in love, and in forgiveness and compassion, I release you. I love me and I release myself from these patterns.'"

I moved to stand opposite the fireplace and I continued talking: "I invite us to remember the support of our mothers and grandmothers. We will put the block of wood in the fire as an expression of agreement to release these patterns and to agree to transform these patterns to something new, for ourselves and for the female lineage of women to come and for those who were before us. All deep energetic work affects seven generations back and seven ahead."

First, Carol stood, with her straight hair, her eyes bright, and said out loud: "I choose and I liberate and I ask for the help of G-d in this release. I release the victimized vulva, the constant clenching that sits in my vagina. I release the fear of death and to be seen in my power. I release the pattern of making myself small. Thank you, thank you, thank you!" She put the wood in the fire and I put a resin of myrrh, which has a strong and powerful purifying quality, in it. Smoke with a delicate yet strong smell rose upwards.

Ellie moved closer with the log in her hand, stood opposite the fire, took a deep breath, and said: "With the support of wonderful creation, I choose and I liberate the victimized vulva. I free myself from the fear of death, the fear of living presently in my body. I release the patterns of belittling myself, the fear of being the sexual woman I am. To the beloved vulva!" Ellie put the block of wood on the fire. I felt awe and great joy from the grace of that moment. Natalie increased the beat of the drum and encouraged the women.

Ruth stood, her body trembling and with tears in her eyes, and said: "Sweet Creator of the world, I implore you: Answer my prayers that come from the depths of my soul. Enough of living my life in subservience! Enough of life as a belittled woman! Enough! I liberate myself from that life. It is about time! Blessed are You, Lord our G-d, Sovereign of all, who has kept us alive, sustained us, and brought us to this moment," she said and threw the log in the fire.

I added more myrrh into the flames, burning what would have been used as incense in the holy temple, and said: "Liberated! Liberated! Liberated!"

Noa stood in front of the flames and held the block of wood in her right hand, resting her other palm on her heart and began to hum, with a sound that ran through the depth of my soul. Her upright stance and her beauty shone throughout the room. She finished singing and said: "I choose and I release myself from the fear of singing my unique song to the world. I convert my shyness and my shame of the sexual woman I am. I choose to live in my full power. I relax and release into being who I am in my fullness, blissfully and peacefully!" She put the log in the fire. It was a moving occasion to see her like this and I exchanged a glance of excitement with Natalie. Noa returned to her place with a spark of the great light in her eyes.

Ember stood in front of the fire, closed her eyes, and took a deep breath: "I am nervous. Please help me. I am terrified."

"We are with you, supporting you in this sacred moment," I assured her.

Ember continued: "In this moment, as witnessed by all these incredible women who are with me here, I choose to release my fear of relationships, the fear of being at ease with who I am next to men, to be in my full presence and power. I release the idea that I am dangerous and able to burn people with my power. I am powerful and that is wonderful! Thank you!" Ember took another deep breath, put her block of wood in the flames, and whispered quietly another few words of prayer to the fire.

Iris stood by the fire. "I have to share this is super strange for me. It's the first time I'm standing in such a way. I choose, from this place of inner strangeness that is coming up within me right now, to give in, to truly dare to let go of this constriction I feel in my heart when facing my husband. I'm fed up with hating him, of being far away from him and from myself. I am fed up with not having sex. This stagnation is over for me. I want love in my life." In a confident voice, if not a little shaky, she carried on: "I release my anger to the fire. I pray to release the fear of being the sexual woman I am, to give her space and expression. I release my fear of love. I choose love in my life! I choose a new balance between the masculine and feminine within me and in my relationship with my husband."

She took a deep breath and added: "Boldly, I set fire to my fear of pleasure and passion. Thank you!" She knelt and put her log on the burning flame. We all stood facing the fire, loving sisters supporting and testifying to her agreement and liberation.

Last to face the fire was Beth. The energy had risen and risen and everyone, as though they felt her unease, stood really close to her. Her expression was full of reverence and holiness, her hair shining from the flames of the fire that burned fiercely, consuming the wood. The light of the flame illuminated her face.

"I am the old woman here in the group who causes all the commotion," she said. "Everyone here enveloped me in so much love. Come even closer to me; it gives me courage."

Everyone drew close to her and she continued: "Do you know what? I have courage, a lot of it, too. I have power. I raised children and grandchildren. I have done much in my life. I have power. You can all step back a little." Everyone took a step back and she carried on: "I, Beth, release the fear of living life in presence in my body and in power. I free my aging vulva that has been through suffering and tension. I release myself from being small! See how much beautiful fat I have? I am so large! I am huge in every sense!" She took the log of wood and threw it into the fire.

The drum and all the women together clapped for her in a standing ovation, clapping for Beth and for themselves. Natalie put tribal music on and we all started to dance jubilantly.

"I am sexual," said Natalie in a funny voice. "I am sexual," she said seriously. "I am sexual," she said with restraint, and she then turned to everyone and instructed: "Play with it."

The room was filled with different versions of that sentence. We danced to the sound of the music happily and together. Beth began to belly dance, moving her hips happily. Ember looked at her joyfully and rolled her shoulders back and forth. Iris danced with small, delicate movements. Ellie stood across from her, looking at her, and started to jump in the air. Iris imitated Ellie's movements and within a few minutes, she also began to jump. The joy of life brought Carol out of her body and her expression was pure happiness.

During the dancing, I noticed Ruth wasn't having an easy time of it. I got closer to her and danced in front of her, with a piercing look into her eyes. She tried to evade my gaze. "What's wrong, Ruth?" I asked.

"What's happening here is just too much for me," she said. "It's way out of my comfort zone, so far that I don't know how to take it." I gave her a hug and Ruth succumbed to it. It's basically all that she wanted: love, care, and attention to her difficulty connecting to the foreignness with which she was all too familiar.

While I hugged her, I whispered in her ear: "It is ok to feel that you don't connect. Love yourself just like that. Let go of the criticism, if it's what is happening right now. Simply let go of it. Let go of the struggle. Yes, great, let go."

Ruth's body went limp and rested in a new way inside my arms. She released and agreed to dissolve more into my arms, giving into the hug. She began to sway gently to the rhythm of the music and untangled herself from the hug of her own accord. Her range of movements expanded and grew, when, suddenly, possibly even surprising herself, a wild, explosive movement jolted her. She devoted herself as though dismantling years of not daring to move her body freely. Our gazes met for a moment and I smiled at her happily.

I carried on dancing, feeling excitement from the sheer magnitude of the occasion. I watched everyone in the room and tears of emotion trickled from my eyes. How much beauty, I marveled; what freedom before me. I whispered a deep prayer for the women on Earth, time, and space to have the freedom to be who they are with ease, where their sexuality is healthy and respected in the world. I said an inner prayer for my male brothers, too, for a life in healthy and balanced sexuality, clean of the porn culture.

Natalie was observing me and saw that I was deep in prayer. She took a few moments until our gazes met, and in the language of our hearts and eyes, we synchronized. It was time to move on to the next stage of the ceremony.

The song finished and Natalie put on a more relaxed song. The beat dropped and, with it, the volume.

"Like that, exactly as you are, stand, spread out your hands, open your faces, bring all of your body to a state where every cell is open and receptive to knowledge. Feel, imagine, sense yourselves like a sponge that can receive a transmission of divine wisdom. It is a knowledge base of creation that is available to all." Natalie continued, "A living book where everything is written since the dawn of the universe. Some call it the Akashic records. You can even turn to the crystal network where the knowledge of life is encoded in the body of Mother Earth. It's on us simply to ask for the knowledge to be made available to us. Repeat after me," she requested. "I, here and now, turn to divine wisdom to bring me back the right to knowledge of life in presence and full power in the body." Everyone repeated after her and I carried on:

"I beseech help from the divine wisdom to clear and cleanse patterns that prevent me from this knowledge. Thanks, thanks, thanks to the knowledge, the wisdom, the insight of the heart, the insight of the vulva, and the wisdom that walks me safely on the ground that is available to me from now on."

The women repeated after me and we all took a deep breath together. Each time, I am surprised anew at how such a clear statement to the universe, to creation, to the g-ds, resonates so very strongly. I meet people, even years after they participated in ceremonies, who emphasize this moment changed their lives.

I was so emotional because I knew in every cell of my being the lives of everyone that would leave this room today would change. For one, it would change with great intensity, for another, more subtly—almost invisible to the naked eye, each one according to her own inner wisdom and pace.

I looked at Natalie. Her presence by me in ceremonies reassures me. It's a huge privilege for me to experience such strength together, to be part of a sisterhood of the heart in a powerful moment such as this. I felt my gratitude and I said: "I am here and now merging the human I am with my divinity."

Electricity of excitement and intensity ran through the air as all the women continued with me and after my words. "I am a complete being," I finished the sentence. Spontaneously, I began to sing, all the while banging on the drum:

"Here I am. I am all yours. Do with me as you wish."

Everyone joined me, some humming, others learning the words as I sang them.

"I came empty. I surrender. Do with me as you wish, even if everything is revoked from me. Within me your voice I hear, even if everything is taken from me. Within me your voice I hear. From the pain G-d rises in me. Fill my heart with your grace. From the pain, G-d rises up in me. Fill my heart with love."

We sang the words over and over, moving closer to one another, until, by the end, we were standing side by side and singing together in strength and holiness. The song finished. We stood hugging, very close to one another.

"Look each other in the eyes," Natalie requested. "See, bear witness to the special spark we see here, in all of your eyes. Guard this special moment in your hearts."

What beauty, I said to myself, what a pleasure that more women choose to develop and be in their sexualities. I met Natalie's eyes. Years of guiding and facilitating ceremonies together had passed between us, a contract of sorority and sisterhood full of support. Each of us were there for one another in challenging moments, to help each other cope and grow courageously and be fully seen in the world. Feelings of deep gratitude flowed between us.

Ruth was looking at the women, searching to meet someone's eyes. Her eyes fell on Carol and a huge smile rose on Carol's face, with so much love and depth. Ruth relaxed, filled with the love that Carol radiated into her eyes with simplicity and ease.

So, too, Noa, who for most of the workshop had kept a low profile, was looking into everyone's eyes. Ember looked at Beth and started to laugh contagiously. Beth cracked a smile, which widened, and eventually laughed with her—for a good few minutes, too, infecting everyone with laughter. Healthy, healing, stimulating, continuous, and endless laughter.

I rode the wave of laughter to bring more women the medicine of liberation and joy through laughter, so there would be more space for ceremonial wisdom to assimilate into the cells of the bodies of each of the women.

"We are closing the ceremony," I said. "Thank you to the centering spirit of the ceremony that was present with us and leading us. You are invited to stay and shine in the hearts of each one of us here. You are released from the ceremony. Thank you, thank you, thank you."

Everyone replied together: "Thank you, thank you, thank you."

Natalie continued: "Thank you to the spirit from below, for giving us steady and sure ground. Thank you, thank you, thank you!"

"Thank you!" they joined with Natalie.

I raised my arms upwards and everyone joined me: "Thank you to the spirit of above for the inspiration and infinite wisdom."

"Thank you to the spirit of the North, to the wisdom of the grandmother. You are freed from the ceremony. Thank you, thank you, thank you!" Natalie said.

I carried on: "Thank you to the spirit of the West, for the support in the purification and letting go of the old. Thank you, thank you, thank you. Released!"

"Thank you to the spirit of the South for the passion and fire of balanced life. Released. Thank you, thank you, thank you!"

Natalie swapped with me and I finished the circle of gratitude by saying: "Thank you to the spirit of the East for the support in giving life to more of our power. Thank you, thank you, thank you!"

"Thank you to each and every one of you for dedicating yourselves here," said Natalie. "Thank you for the cooperation, for the trust that you placed in us and in each other, and for your daring to bring more of yourselves. It's not a given that you would do that."

"I invite everyone to take a few moments to themselves," I said. "If something comes up for you and you want to write it down, write it in your notebooks. Go to the bathroom and we'll meet back at the sharing circle in a few minutes. Come, let's take some time to ourselves in silence, without small talk, but hugs are allowed and recommended!"

Ember let go of her need to escape outside and take deep

breaths of nicotine, and lay on the mattress. Beth took a chair and sat close to Ember. An unspoken agreement had been forged between them despite the large age gap.

Carol laid down on a mattress and breathed deeply as she rested her hands on her lower stomach. Noa sat next to her crossed-legged, closing her eyes and sitting in meditation.

I went to bring a bowl of dates and almonds to pass it between the women to snack on. I sat, breathing deeply, absorbing the frequency that was passing through me throughout the ceremony.

*I choose. I agree. I walk calmly in my sexual power. I am sexual!*

*Here and now, I relinquish my vows that I have taken throughout my life, in all the worlds, times, dimensions, and levels. I relinquish the vows that prevented me from living a balanced life between the masculine and feminine within me, and in my relationships, vows that prevented me from having full presence in my body and for my life in power. I am here and now and I choose and reclaim my right to live in presence and in my full power.*

*I choose to live in balance and honor between the masculine and feminine inside me and in a renewed partnership between male and female.*

*In gratitude and with the loving support of the wonderful creator, I choose and let go of the victimized vulva. I let go of the fear of being present in my body. I let go of the patterns of making myself small. Cheers to the beloved vulva!*

*I am here and now, turning to divine wisdom and reclaiming the right to knowledge of life in presence and full power in my body. I ask for support from divine wisdom in cleansing and releasing patterns that prevent me from accessing this knowledge. Thank you, thank you, thank you for the knowledge, the wisdom, the wisdom from the heart, the wisdom from the womb, the wisdom from the vulva, and the wisdom of walking safely on this Earth. They are all available to me from now on.*

*I am here and now, merging the human I am with my divinity. I am a whole being.*

# SHARING CIRCLE

Ten minutes later, all the women had returned to sit in the circle. Ruth arrived last, smiling, yet slightly embarrassed, and sat next to Iris. Even Noa, who kept herself separate from everyone else for the most part, sat close to Ellie. There was a shared desire to stay close together and still feel the powerful experience they had just gone through a short time ago.

"How are you all, dears? Would anyone like to share?" I asked as I looked around lovingly and compassionately to each of the participants.

"I will start," Beth opened the circle. "First of all, I want to say a personal thank you to each of you. I experienced absolute terror, a genuine, paralyzing fear. I have no words to even describe what I went through and you were all just there for me. Your touch, the singing.... In my entire life, I've never gone through anything like it. It was a defining moment for me; I will never forget it. Thank you so much! I want to share I do feel I have a chance I'll have sex, or, how Michal likes to put it, make love, and it won't hurt me. This is the first time I feel like such a chance exists. I am excited by the very idea that it's even possible!"

"Thank you, Beth," said Natalie. "May you have full faith that it is possible. May you expand from inside and relax your vulva even more.

"I have much more to release regarding my vagina," said Beth. "Only now, I have begun to understand just how tightly she was constricted. Generations upon generations of constriction. I think even my mother had a clenched vagina, and definitely my grandmother, if how she talked about my grandfather is anything to go by," Beth finished.

"I want us to contemplate the way we think and express ourselves in regard to our relationships," I said, and Natalie added: "Don't avoid things that bother or trigger and annoy you. Treat those things with the utmost attention and examine in depth what exactly is lying beneath those complaints. What is your soul yearning for? Do not neglect yourselves. You are the most important thing in the world."

"Come on, be real. I'm the most important thing in the world? Trump is the most important; look at how much influence he has," Ember said in defiance.

"You are the most important woman in the world," repeated Natalie. "You are the center of your world."

"Everything is a reflection of each one of us. What we think, feel, and do in this world has a direct effect on our reality," I said. "Each one of us is the center of her own world and her creator. The more men and women understand they are the center of their world, and who take responsibility for their center, the better it will be for them, and the world will be a much better place!"

"I have no words to describe what I'm feeling right now," said Ruth, her blonde hair shining and complexion glowing. "I feel relieved, compassionate for myself. It's the first time I truly feel that I am worth something. Truly, without anyone telling me I am from the outside. The experience of making myself small for men is such a strong one in my life that even when I got divorced, I felt so small and like a complete failure. Each time anew I am astounded at this other person would come and control me. Why did that happen to me in such a powerful way?"

"It's connected to the pattern of master and slave," I said, "a pattern that we carry in our collective memories. It's a force that leads to many interactions between men and women in a very covert and unconscious way. When we find balance between and honor the feminine and masculine energies within us, that, in turn, reflects on our relationships, too. I hold ceremonies of forgiveness between the male and female. It's a formative ritual that I recommend to everyone to experience or create for themselves. What we did today, to choose a life in full presence and full power in our bodies , is part of the deep process of changing the balance of power between male and female, from war to partnership."

"When you forgive," added Natalie, "you allow for the creation of new communication and agreement to a life of peace based on honoring the masculine and feminine. Therefore, the vulva can rest, relax, and contain even more."

"Thank you," said Ruth. "I only hope I will be able to implement all that in my daily life."

"You will leave here with clear instructions on what to do. Fulfillment of those actions is entirely up to each of you," I said and looked with a loving and trusting look upon the participants. "We will give you guidance as to how to put them into action, helping support you and enabling this change in your lives.

"From my own experience, I recognize that feeling where I know exactly what to do to instigate a change in my life and when a force within me seeks to stop me from moving forward or advancing. At the same time, I am conscious of my inner power that allows me to start fresh. It takes inner determination, perseverance, and a constant cleansing of any obstacles that prevent me from developing." I closed my eyes for a moment and prayed for the women to find that strength, to create and to instigate changes in their lives.

As I opened my eyes, Ember said, all the while looking straight into Beth's eyes: "I want to tell you that you really touched my heart. Thank you for trusting me and agreeing to accept my support. You didn't have to do that, but you did," she said, tears running down her cheeks.

Beth put her hand on Ember. "Sometimes I feel like I have so much knowledge, wisdom, and the ability to help people and I just stop myself and smother that desire to give, needing nothing in return," said Ember. "Lending support to you came to me so easily. From the moment, we met I felt that click with you, one of those connections that doesn't need words, one that forgoes the need to tell you about myself or my dramatic stories. The fact that such straightforward love is out there is so wonderful."

"It's wonderful for me, too. I think I would have died if you weren't next to me," said Beth.

Ember smiled at her with a loving look and said: "I want to say thanks for the ceremony. I stood in front of the fire with that wood in my hand, with a resolute intention and genuine request for support in cleansing patterns that created a tense reality around my sexuality and in my communication with men in general. I am so good at creating drama all around me. I put that wood in the fire, silently. I am used to sharing stories about men with my girlfriends. But I am fed up with being the one with all the drama. I really hope I can meet a man who I am able to be truly relaxed with, from the inside—peaceful, with an empowered vulva. I want to be comfortable with who I am, to stop stressing about my sexual experiences. To fly, to be happy, to enjoy my sexuality, without needing to talk about it with the entire world. How lucky I listened and came to the workshop with the weird name," finished Ember.

After a moment of silence, Iris joined in: "It was really emotional for me. I've never been in a ceremony like that one. At least, not in this life. It was all new to me and yet, I felt so very at home. The smell of the sage, the drum, the special energy that was created between us. I felt the place was bewitched, in a good way, a really good way! I want more ceremonies like that in my life, truly. Thank you," said Iris.

I waited quietly for the next person who wanted to share. After a few moments, Ellie began to talk: "My deep understanding was that I take more responsibility in my choices over what and who I let inside me. Even though I managed before, well, at least relatively, now I feel subtle nuances that I've never paid attention to before. It could be with someone I loved who I slept with a million times and suddenly, today, his touch just doesn't feel right. I learned to succeed in finding the power to say no, to listen more to my body and to really remember that my body knows. And if a contraction arises in my body, I stop. It's about time that I stop avoiding it. I never knew how to say no or to stop situations where I really didn't want to be in a sexual circumstance. For a few months now, I've been in a relationship with a married man. I've been stressing about it from here to Jerusalem, full of guilt. None of my friends know he is married. I feel I must release this secret. G-d, it's so heavy to carry around!"

Ember looked at her lovingly and said: "It's good that you unloaded this secret from your shoulders. Maybe now you will feel a bit lighter!" she said as she got up to hug Ellie, staying to sit close to her.

"Thank you, Ellie love, for sharing that secret," I said. "Secrets weaken us and waste a lot of our energy. You've brought up a complicated subject. If it makes you feel any better, you should know that chances are most women have been attracted to another man who is not her partner, and the same goes for men towards other women. The question is what we do with that attraction and if there is something hidden around it, because hiding is one of the biggest ways our energy can be stolen—it's the biggest energy thief there is. Let's remember it's okay to experience ourselves as sexual in the world. Our responsibility is to hone in on who we choose to establish sexual relations with, to ask ourselves honestly, what truly supports us in our lives? To walk with your inner compass of integrity, to be very, very wise, loving, and compassionate, first of all towards, yourselves and towards those around you. I think at the core of our existence, we are not monogamous creatures. We live in a society that has been living monogamously for generations. The collapse of the monogamous structure can be very painful. It asks us for maximum sensitivity, honesty, and sisterhood that really isn't suitable for everyone."

Suddenly, Noa got up and went to sit on the other side of Ellie, saying: "I want to give you a hug." Noa hugged her, as Ember's hand was still resting on Ellie's back. Ellie smiled gratefully, all the while looking at me as she was hugged by Noa and Ember.

"You've made the first step into coming out of hiding. I invite you to cleanse yourself of the shame and feelings of guilt and to ask the creator to help you unravel your inner entanglements inside you. Only then can you create for yourself the reality you wish for in your life, to live in peace, in integrity, and inner joy. Again, I want to congratulate you for speaking out about it. I am sure you already feel a little relieved!" I smiled at her lovingly. "Is there anyone else who wants to add anything before we close today and go to take a sweet and beneficial sleep?" I asked.

Noa let go of hugging Ellie and said: "I know that I haven't spoken or shared for almost the entire day. Usually, I don't speak and share what I am feeling, but this time, given your request to change our patterns, I decided to talk. Sexuality is not something I am comfortable with. I was never really taught to access my sexuality, or to talk about it, or even understand what to do with it. Everything I know is from experience and mistakes that would sometimes pay off and be pleasant and sometimes be very disappointing. I have been in a relationship for a few years now and our sex life isn't really the main ingredient in it. We really love each other, but we hardly ever manage to find the time to engage in the sacred act of love. I want that to change and I think he wants that, too. And both of us want children. Even talking about this out loud is making it easier. I never spoke about it with anyone. The ritual awakened my choice to be more daring, to learn, to ask, to try, to expand my knowledge around sexuality, and, mainly, to start to talk about it more openly with my boyfriend. I believe this is a good start and certainly something has stirred within me. Let's see where it will take me!"

We all looked at her, at her angelic face with such sweet, innocent eyes, her flowing blond hair, her softness extending to her every word, which was like sprinkling fairy dust throughout the room.

"Thank you," I said, "for being able to share with us even though it wasn't easy for you. May you make those children from a place of happy sexuality, love, and pleasure. Children who are born from a happy, loving sexual union begin life from a more beneficial place."

I looked at Natalie, feeling like that was the end. We arrived at the time to go to sleep. I saw she was feeling exactly the same way.

"It was so lovely to be a guest at your ceremony," said Natalie. "It was my privilege to be with you in such a special moment and I am so grateful for it."

"Thank you, Natalie, for being you," I said after she spoke. "It's always so incredible to do a ceremony with you." I observed the women and said: "It's time to go to sleep. We'll meet in the morning at eight for an hour-long yoga lesson and at 9:15, there will be breakfast. I recommend you all to go to sleep. We had a full day, and much of the work to process what we learned continues at night."

I hugged Natalie lovingly and gave thanks for our endless partnership on this journey of life. Natalie packed her belongings and returned home. The women dispersed to their bedrooms. I stayed alone in the room, closing the day, saying thanks to the creator for supporting us on this busy day, to the rain that fell in abundance, to the fire that was lit in the hearth, to Mother Earth for hosting us, and to the space for the wonderful support. By then, I was so tired. I gathered the last of my strength to tidy the room so it would be ready for the yoga practice in the morning. I went to my room, lit the kettle for tea, and laid down on my bed. My body was so happy to lie down and rest. In these situations, when I am exhausted, I either fall asleep immediately or it takes a moment to digest everything I had been through. I felt this time, I needed to take a moment to digest. I prepared myself a delicious cup of winter tea made of cinnamon and a little honey. I held the cup in my palms, enjoying the treat of the heat. I took a calming breath, relaxing on the armchair, and gazed at the wall, taking a moment with myself to rest and soak in what had happened during the day. Now and again, a picture would arise in my mind and I let the pictures pass by as I returned myself to quiet awareness. I laid down to rest and fell asleep fast.

*I, here and now, choose and allow myself time to assimilate, rest, and relax. Thank you!*

# MOUTH —VAGINA — ANUS

I woke up fifteen minutes before my alarm clock, giving me a little more time to snuggle in bed. The winter sun shone through the window and everything sparkled and shined, in complete contrast to the grayness of yesterday. I took a few deep breaths, blessed myself and the new day, got up from bed, and went to wash my face and drink water. I am used to getting up straight away into making sandwiches, lunch boxes, and helping do whatever each of my kids asks of me. I love them so very much. They, without doubt, are the greatest teachers of my life. The mornings where I wake up alone without the children are rare.

I did a short yoga exercise to prepare for the day, with a prayer that I be given the opportunity to hand the women the tools to soak in change and meaning into their lives; so that they may have a happier sex life and greater life force and vitality in their day to day lives. I asked for the support of the universe. I took a deep breath and a long exhale. I went outside to breathe fresh air. Everything glittered outside. The winter sunlight shone on the raindrops that saturated the grass, the leaves, and the soil. Saturated. I took more deep breaths and felt the fresh, cold air enter my lungs and fill me with life force. I returned to the meeting space turned on the air conditioner, as I didn't feel like dealing with the fire

I prepared myself a cup of tea and lit the incense in the room, with the intention of purifying the space around me as I turned around in a spiral. I stood in the center of the yurt and suddenly, I realized that a yoga class was not what the group was asking for. Free movement in the space to pleasing music and sounds was far more suitable. Instead of a circle of yoga mats, I created a circle of pillows.

First to enter was Noa, who sat down. I smiled at her to wish her good morning. The sun illuminated the room. The space was so different from the gray of the day before. The rest of the women came in and most of them hugged one another hello.

"Good morning," I said as I grinned widely. Everyone answered me, smiling, and it was so nice to see how they all lit up. I carried on talking: "I hope you all slept well. You look refreshed and beaming this morning. It gives me so much pleasure to see you all like this, with a new spark within you. Yesterday, I thought this morning we would practice yoga, but I woke up with a certain clarity that it's more suitable to dance. Whoever feels like doing yoga stretches is welcome to mix the movement into their free and personal practice. I hope the last-minute change is a welcome one for you!"

Ember smiled and said: "Of course. Dancing is the most fun!"

The women got up, each one moving the pillow they had sat on to the side of the room. Noa came to me and asked:

"I see that the fire hasn't been lit this morning. Maybe, instead of dancing, I could light the fire and then dance with it?"

My heart filled with joy that she had been daring enough to bring to me her genuine desire.

"Of course, you are most welcome! Please greet the fire when you light it so that it will impart warmth upon us all and kindle desire within us."

Noa gazed at me with a profound look in her blue eyes. "I've never lit a fire before with such a blessing, but I'm willing to try." I responded with a look of thanks. I went to the sound system, connected my phone, and put on my favorite playlist that I like to use in workshops. Pleasant music with the sound of an Indian flute filled the space.

"Let's stand together in a circle. We will have a little distance from each other," I said. Everyone took a step back and the circle widened. "Spread your arms and see that you have enough space to move freely," I continued to guide the circle.

The sun lit their faces and, besides the hearth, Noa was preparing the fire. I went to her and whispered to her to prepare everything to light the fire and when she felt she was ready to light it, to signal to me. "We will light the fire with the common intention of everybody together," I told her. She smiled at me, satisfied.

I was delighted with the pleasant clarity that flowed through me. I love to receive the wisdom of the moment as it guides me and fine-tunes me to every new moment. The women had begun to move naturally to the sounds of the music.

"Good morning to our lovely bodies," I said. "Let's take a few deep breaths, everyone according to their own needs. I invite you all, at the same time as your deep breathing, to identify what movement your bodies are asking to make now to awaken and move you!"

I devoted myself to the sounds of the flute that moved me gently and softly. To my joy, I saw that everyone had given themselves easily into the music. Noa looked at me, signaling that she was ready to light the fire. I invited her with a hand gesture to join us in moving freely. She sat on the floor crossed-legged and took a few deep breaths, trying to connect to the process. Ember was rolling slowly on the floor and Iris sat with her legs stretched out. The record changed and the beat increased a little.

"Okay, dears, you came to the workshop to empower and to release your vulva," I said. "Start moving your hips right and left, back and forward, around in circles; feel what works for you. Place one hand on your vaginal area, on your lower stomach, or on the sides of your hips and feel whatever movement that area is asking you to make. That is the source of our life."

Gentle, Oriental-style music played, awakening and moving our hips naturally.

I watched Beth in astonishment at the freedom with which her pelvis moved. I looked at Ruth and saw the usual stiffness in her hips, but even then, her movement was slightly freer. She circled her hips and even cracked a smile.

I was so pleased. I said: "Bring life to your hips. Move them to awaken them and bring life." I felt the energy rise. I handed out handkerchiefs and signaled that they should tie them around their hips. The handkerchiefs brought them more awareness and more freedom to their movements.

"When the vulva is empowered and free, your hips are more open and relaxed. The gates of life become more available, wider, easier to access," I continued. "Keep moving. I invite you to listen to me with your energetic bodies and less from your ears and minds. When you sleep well, the body is relaxed, rested, released, and sinks into deep sleep. You begin to dream, to hover between infinite dimensions and worlds, where the soul moves within and between them as entire worlds become revealed to you. So, too, the yoni

is moving between dimensions, the space between the material and the spiritual worlds. When you are relaxed, she is released and comfortably able to pass between those dimensions and experience the infiniteness that she is."

Much of the time, I am afraid of sharing the higher knowledge that comes through me. I'm not always sure that what I am saying will be understood and that my words are clear enough. This morning, I felt it was okay, that my words would enable them to move more freely, and I felt I had permission to continue.

"When you are free in your sexual being, the sexual energy flows through you and supports you. So, too, if you are a married woman and you feel your sexual energy rise for another man, you can breathe, expand, smile, and relax. Receive the energy that passes through the vulva and body calmly, with love. It's more life energy that flows in our bodies. When we are less stressed and pressured over our sexual energy, more life and vitality will enter our bodies.

"When you agree and accept your sexual power into your life, the powerful, vital life force will pass through you and you will be more open to the possibilities of fulfillment in your lives.

More power will be made available for you. Let the movement, the pleasure of the body that is derived from the movement, come into being and be within you."

I knew some of the women didn't even hear my words and others caught just part of what I said. I strongly feel that the energetic language passes on the energy behind my words, working as intended. The music intensified and they started dancing in joy and delight. It was a morning of celebration and a celebration of life, of female energy frolicking together.

"I ask now that we move the pelvis with our awareness of our anuses, which sits among the circular muscle systems of the mouth and the vagina," I continued. "I invite you, as you do the following movement, to move your mouth. Contract and release together with the ring muscles of your hips. Feel your anuses and what it wants to say to you...."

I looked and examined their reactions. In the past, I used to be scared to talk about the anus. It's not at all comfortable to talk about the anus in plural form.

Beth looked at me and said: "Oh, please, enough... Now, you've gone too far. It's a workshop to empower our vulvas, not to empower my ass or assehole, or in the medical term, rectum. You really have crossed my limit."

I smiled at her and requested: "Just carry on dancing. I see you really know how to move your bottom. What do you care about being aware of its opening?"

"What do I care? You are the first person in my entire life to ask me to pay attention to my anus. Next thing you know, you'll be telling me to breathe into it," she said and everyone burst out laughing with her.

Beth carried on: "Rest your hand on your bottoms—excuse me, on the opening that is in your bottoms and breathe into him. Great, you are all amazing!" she said mockingly. With all the laughter I felt that this was a moment to pick up on her words, so, in an effort to help her connect with herself, I said:

"Thank you for bringing the spirit of fun and laughter, because, like I said, laughter releases us in our vaginas and also our anuses. Thank you for helping us release a little more."

Beth smiled and looked at me with understanding. I felt that she was agreeing to give into something different and perhaps a little embarrassing for her.

I continued: "All of you move your hips in a spiral, like the letter 'pey' in Hebrew, a letter that is in constant spiraling motion." As I spoke, I moved my hands in a continuous spiral. "We will go in and out of the circle in a spiral. I suggest we hold hands for a moment, so it will be easier to understand."

They held hands and I led the movement inwards in a clockwise spiral direction and then outwards, counterclockwise. We went in and out and all the while, I continued to explain: "The circular muscles in the vagina, the mouth, and the anus are all connected on many levels.[11] The mouth is the entrance of our digestive system and ends with the exit—the anus. The circular muscles directly connect those two openings. Tension that accumulates in the mouth, in the jaw, directly affects the anus, the vagina, or both."

We all continued to move in a spiral and then I asked: "Let go of each other's hands and move freely around the room in the movement of the spiral or the circular muscles. As you do this movement, contract and release your anal muscles and place your awareness in that area."

They let go of each other's hands. Ember started to rotate around the room similar to the Sufi dance, where one stands on a certain point and twirls around while the hands are spread out wide. Iris moved in wider circles that flowed through the entire length of the yurt. Ruth played between the two, one moment

---

11. 'Pey' letters. In Hebrew, the words for vagina, mouth, and anus begin with this the same letter, 'pey.' Vagina is 'pot,' mouth is 'peh,' and anus is 'pi ha-taba'at.' The letter pey is much like the English 'p.' The letter pey has the shape of a spiral like the circular muscles.

twirling in place and the other widening and expanding her movements.

I looked and admired the liberating movement and said: "I remind you all that the anus is a blessed and important organ that supports us and allows the release of everything that is no longer necessary. It can function as a released, flaccid organ that moves freely and comfortably, but equally it can be constricted, contracted, tight and unable to release. It's possible to go to the bathroom and take a relaxed bowel movement with no effort at all or it's possible to need a lot of effort. Keep moving and find that release and freedom within the movement, the freedom to release and let go."

I saw Beth let go and release into a free and contented movement—a familiar movement that is at the base of her being, that she hadn't danced for years. I looked at Carol and saw that she was finding it challenging. I sent her loving energy from my heart to hers. I spoke to everyone, but I felt this time, my words were directed and focused on her. "The anus is an organ that holds gentle and constant tension between contraction and release. Anyone who has ever experienced hemorrhoids knows just how much life's stresses, which accumulate in the anus, take this organ out of balance and bring a lot of pain and suffering." Something changed in Carol's face and I felt that she knew what I was talking about. Her movement changed. More inner freedom was born; I saw it being created in a fraction of a second by her choice. Hallelujah!

I said: "Great, continue to move in a spiral, focusing on the circular muscles of the anus, which are the base of our core muscles. Contracting the ring muscles awakens us to awareness of our core—to the center of our body and the center of our being. If it's comfortable for you to do so, continue moving in a spiral as you collect and release the circular muscles. Keep going, but you can also stand in one place and focus on contracting and releasing.

"The anus has a primary and central role in waste disposal. The direct connection to the anus and vagina muscles greatly influences the act of love and facilitates pleasure. To achieve a full release of the vagina, we need the skills and agreement also to free the anus. When both these areas agree to this, magic happens. Our endless beings ask us to connect to our physical body. The anus is a great gate to pleasure. It is a spiraling, circular mouth that allows another channel of communication to open up to you. It's so important to be in contact and communication with the anus, to pay attention when you relax it, when you contract it, and what she wants to say to you. The anus is a deep force to root us to the ground as a stable anchor, strong and clear on the ground. An anus in balance grants us basic security of existence. The anus is a significant point of contact with our physical existence.

"The anus reflects our ability to know when to hold on and when to let go, to feel comfortable with holding and comfortable with releasing. When there is discomfort in the anus, the whole area will be tense."

The rhythm of the music increased a little. Everyone moved a little more freely in her body. I really saw how their hips were becoming freer with the motion, how ease and comfort were becoming part of their movement, and I said: "Let us put an intention together. You are welcome to say it in your hearts and to present it here and now into the movement of your bodies: I choose to walk on the Earth calmly." I took a deep breath and gave them a moment to be present with the choice in movement. I continued: "We are activating the intention. You are invited to dance it, to be in it, or simply to say it quietly in your hearts as you move. I choose and I live in awareness and attentiveness to my anus. I agree and I let go of the holding and heavy load that sits on my anus. I move freely, I agree, and I release what isn't necessary." Ruth's movement portrayed renewed freedom. It made me so happy. Ellie danced delicately and calmly, making me feel as though her movements were caressing my heart. I let this free, tranquil, and powerful movement be present in the room for a few more moments.

Slowly, but surely, I turned down the volume of the music

and we returned to the quiet flute music as I asked each one of the women to take a mattress, lie down on her back, and relax. Alongside the melody of the flute, I played on the crystal bowls. I felt the vibration of the crystal touch the passageways to their souls.

"Touch the tip of your tongue to the roof of your mouths," I said as I guided them into deep relaxation, "eyes slack, sinking into the eye sockets, eyebrows separated to the sides, your body limp and sinking towards the ground. Place your attention to the points where your body is in contact with the Earth and consent to letting go and relaxing even further. Remember that when you relax your jaw, so, too, your vagina relaxes."

The music stopped. We could hear the wind whispering outside. From that quiet place, we heard the noise of the air conditioner and I remembered how much I had wanted to light a pleasant fire in the fireplace. After a few minutes of quiet I spoke: "Bring your awareness back to your breath." I saw Carol deepen her breath and so, too, did Ruth.

"Place your hands on your vaginal area and breathe into her," I instructed. "Feel her, feel the simple expression of the woman you are, your femininity. Inhale deeply into the anus and feel the connection between the anal muscles and the vaginal muscles. I invite you to breathe the energy of peace to the vagina, peace with the anus, peace with your sexuality. We agree and we bring back the life force into our own hands, so that we may have more life force to create our desired reality."

I gave the women a few minutes of quiet and serenity. "Beloveds, take another deep breath and gently move your hands and feet." I waited a moment before carrying on. "Bring your legs together. Bring your hands to your head and stretch from the tips of your fingers to the tips of your toes. Roll onto your right side and come back to a seated position."

Slowly, one by one, they sat up. Carol opened her eyes and said: "What a wonderful start to the morning!"

"I am already pretty hungry for breakfast," said Ember.

"Yes, totally," I said as a smile rose on my lips. "This morning, we will enjoy a royal breakfast that Rose prepared for us."

Rose popped her head inside from the kitchen next door and I gestured for her to come in. "Just one more minute," I requested. "Let's light the fire in the hearth. Rose, come join us. Noa, you are invited to light the fire. I invite you all to light with her with the intention that this is the fire of life, one that brings good and beneficial medicine to our sexuality for more peace within ourselves and between the sexes."

Ember applauded, "Yes!" and everyone nodded in agreement as Noa lit the fire.

"Let's go eat breakfast," I said.

*I choose to live in awareness of the connection across my mouth, my vagina, and my anus. Relaxation is more present in my life. Thank you!*

*I choose to breathe the energy of peace to the vagina, to the anus, and to my sexual being. I agree and I allow more life force to flow through me!*

*I choose to agree and I accept into my life the sexual power and the vital life force that flows through me.*

We sat together around the table and laughed. We spoke a lot about femininity, about vulvas and releasing the vagina. While we were having breakfast, I received clarity. I felt the moment had come to talk and to enrich the quality of the male energy. After all, women and men carry both masculine and feminine qualities inside themselves.

I went out to breathe the sunny winter air. Despite the morning sun, the trees were wet and the earth saturated. Noa also stood outside and I put my hand gently on her shoulder to ask her how she was.

She smiled and answered: "Everything that has gone on here has far exceeded my expectations. It's so very deep and enlightening. It makes me aware of places I never even thought existed within me. I am really grateful to you for that. Michal, you are heartwarming and touching in the candor and authenticity you bring to everything you do. You are so inspiring. Thank you!"

I smiled and looked into her eyes lovingly, with so much gratitude. I gave her a warm hug and after a few moments, I moved my head a little, looking at her and saying: "The most important thing is for you to feel comfortable with who you are so that you will be sure of your steps on this Earth, because insecurity no longer serves you. I have the feeling you have a lot more to give to the world. The world wants to hear your voice. It's a wonderful and much needed voice to hear in the world!"

She smiled. "Thank you. I feel the ceremony yesterday cleansed something deep from inside me and I have more courage."

"I already felt that this morning, when I asked you to light the fire," I answered her, smiling as I walked away. I felt that I needed a moment to myself. I sat on a rock under the sun and I warmed up from the winter rays, letting them recharge me. I prayed for more help to bring clear words and supportive energy for the completion of the workshop. I know everyone has their own pace for their journeys and in their abilities to implement things. I prayed that each one, in her own way, receive at least one meaningful thing in her life because of this workshop.

*I choose to allow the new information that is coming to me to be embedded in each and every cell in my body, in the right place for me. Thank you!*

# MASCULINE ENERGY

I went back inside. I asked everyone to join me. I smiled and said: "Well, I hope everyone had a tasty and nutritious breakfast. Until now, we leaned into conversation about the vulva. I want to talk for a moment about the penis and about masculine energy. I am waiting for the man who will write the book "Relax the Penis."

Everyone smiled. Ember said: "I thought about it another way: when the penis is flaccid, the vagina can let go."

Beth looked at her in astonishment and said: "The penis is not supposed to be flaccid when it goes in, and truthfully, it's a real downer if it's limp when you really feel like doing it. It simply doesn't work... and then everyone is frustrated—the man and the woman."

To my surprise, Ruth retorted: "Beth, I don't think that's what Ember and Michal meant. Maybe the intention was for something calmer and that it doesn't want to enter straight away, finish, and leave?"

"Both of you have said the right things," I answered. "In the beginning, the statement 'relax the penis' raises a smile. On face value, the penis is supposed to be erect. I use the concept of a freed, released, or limp penis; it means the penis is less goal-orientated, so that when the penis approaches the act of love, it agrees to be on hold, in breath, in relaxation, and allows things to happen over a slower process. A woman needs 20 minutes until the life fluid begins to awaken and to be ready for penetration. A released penis has the patience to wait and maybe derives pleasure from the intimacy of being present in the moment," I finished my speech.

"Sometimes, I, as a woman, am as goal-oriented as the penis and all I want is to reach orgasm," said Iris, surprisingly.

"Maybe the intention is to let go of this matter of men who are goal-oriented and only interested in penetrating me," Carol continued the line of thought.

"Pornographic movies just distort the sexuality. Men don't have any clue how to touch sensitively, how to pay attention to what the woman is really asking for. I'm pretty tired of that."

"Wait a minute," Ember burst out, "don't generalize! There are men that know how to touch and listen to a woman's body."

"I have no doubt deep healing seeks to come through here," I said. "It's a process. It takes time to change deeply embedded patterns that are encoded in our society. When each one takes responsibility for herself, she will influence those around her. I invite you to experiment next time and allow yourselves to let something else happen in sexual situations. Be full of passion and pleasure, but less goal-orientated, with a desire for connection, simplicity, and the magic of presence. Let's finish talking here and stand up."

I stood up and everyone stood up after me. "We will walk around the room however we feel to do so, experiencing the masculine energy that resides in us."

I began to walk freely and they joined in. "Walk around the space as though we own a male chest, inflated and expanded." All of them suddenly straightened up and their shoulders rose. I kept talking: "Imagine your male organ, the penis. Feel it as a protruding organ from your loins. Imagine the testicles."

They continued to walk around the room and their presence in the space changed. "Stay focused on your penis[12] — be present with the feeling of confusion of masculine energy and feel what happens to you."

Something in Beth's stance was contracted and the same thing was apparent in Ruth, too. "Be with the *bulbul* more," I said,

12. One of the words in Hebrew for penis is 'bulbul,' which has in it the Hebrew word for confusion, 'bilbul' and also the Hebrew word to be on target, 'bul.'

adding: "You can also be *bul*—meaning on target—twice, making *bul-bul*, which means to aim exactly at the target. It is really on point, with precision and a clear power that knows exactly what it wants and is ready and willing to do everything to obtain it. Look into each other's eyes as you walk around the space and you all know exactly what your goals are. Feel it."

The room filled with testosterone, a celebration of masculinity. I said: "Okay, stop."

Everyone froze in their male stance. "Take a deep breath and think of a word that demonstrates the feeling you experienced."

Ember said immediately: "Power."

Beth said: "I feel like getting in a fight with everyone."

Noa said: "I liked it. It was kind of powerful softness."

Iris said: "I feel like superman or superwoman."

"Take another breath into this male experience that you feel now in your body," I requested.

"I have the need to move already," said Ember. "To be frozen like this doesn't fit my masculinity."

"Right," I said. "Male energy is in movement. So move with it, but this time, with mindfulness."

A palpable air of softness was now present in the room. They walked around the room, with sharpened senses, focused, yet with a lot more comfort in the body. It was so very nice to see it. I said: "A flaccid penis can also be erect, but with a conscious, patient mind. With presence and relaxation while erect. And now, stop, take a deep breath, and be with that thought."

I waited a moment. I felt the silence honored this moment. Spoken words would only disturb the deep and present feeling in the room, the feeling of a new and deep understanding that relaxation and power can work together.

After a few long moments of silence, Ember said: "I have to share: It's my understanding that a released, limp, and empowered penis can actually only encounter another vulva that is also

173

released and limp. If she is goal-oriented like the penis, it's almost as though the penis is meeting with another penis."

"When the released and relaxed vagina connects with a limp penis, miracles can occur," I agreed with her. "New electricity is created, much more flows between them, and the energy is more relaxed. Much more pleasure can enter these spaces. The woman consenting to contain inside her a relaxed penis receives the gift of presence and comfort. She receives the quiet, the magic of the encounter from a place of rest; the medicine of love from a place of desire to be and to give and not to gain something. She can experience this in fullness."

Ruth shifted uncomfortably and said: "When you say flaccid penis, is it hard or not? I don't understand how it's possible to make love with a man who doesn't have an erection," she said with a smile as her face turned red.

I knew that it would be really hard for Ruth to put herself in the center, to say that she doesn't understand and to ask such a question. I thanked her in my heart for her courage. I smiled at her and looked her straight in the eye: "Let's put it out there: in order for the penis to enter into a vagina, it has to be hard. What I mean beyond that is the male genitalia, that beautiful and noble thing, has a miraculous presence that knows exactly what it wants. A hard sex organ means when it wants to enter a vagina, it respects the woman's rhythm and pace, with patience and a desire to connect; to be a friend and to give love before entering the vagina; and also keep giving love all the while that it is inside her. It is a lingam that stands firm, clear and connected to the heart, with sensitive attentiveness, who feels himself and the woman he is with. The heart's eye is found at the tip of his penis and radiates love inside the woman.

When the penis is actually inside the woman, he is able to be physically relaxed and continue to pleasure the woman. He is able to merge with the softness of the vagina, where there is a consistent game between the softness of the vagina and the stiffness of the penis."

Beth entered the discussion: "Although I haven't had full sex with penetration for a long time, but from what I remember, I couldn't stand it when my husband stayed inside me after he came."

I smiled and said: "True, that happens, too."

I asked them to continue the conversation while seated. We waited while Ember returned from the toilet. I said: "I want to further expand on the essence of the masculine energy. One of the main roles of the penis is to nourish the vagina.,[13] Part of the masculine transformation is the ability to transform the energy of the warrior into energy that nourishes the woman he is with.

"That's fascinating," Ellie interjected. "The first man I was with, really, I experienced that he was alighting and nourishing me. Every time we made love, I left bursting with energy for a few days. Sometimes, he would even tell me what energy he was charging me with. It was a really uplifting experience."

Beth spoke over her as though she couldn't resist: "You're a lucky girl. You're 20 years old and already experienced such a thing. I think I never had anything like that in my entire life, dear G-d. What did I miss? I think I missed something serious in every way when it comes to sex."

"But did you recognize the experience of elation from pleasant sex?" I asked, and when she nodded, I carried on: "This elation of spirit has many layers and depths to be reached. It's never too late. Invite it into your life...."

"First of all, may my fluids come back," she said sadly, "so I can do it at all."

"I recommend that you research and learn about appropriate practices," I said. "For example, nipple massages, the use of a love egg—an egg-shaped crystal that is placed inside the vagina and, with appropriate exercises, can strengthen the muscles of

---

13. In Hebrew, the word penis – 'zayin,' includes the Hebrew word for weapon and the word for nourishment.

the vaginal canal and the pelvic floor. There are more exercises to strengthen the circular muscles throughout the entire body. All these make the return of the flow of life fluids to your vagina possible."

I knew I had given a lot of information in one go, but I added: "I invite you to continue your journey to acquire knowledge," and Beth's face softened. "We will go back to the penis," I continued. "As I said to you all yesterday, in Sanskrit, the word for penis is *lingam* and the meaning is 'rod of light.'"

Beth once again interjected: "'Rod of light?' Come on, seriously."

I smiled at her. I began to feel discomfort in my body from her comments. I took a deep breath. I knew it stemmed from embarrassment, fear, and lack of knowledge. While breathing, I turned to the universe and asked for help to allow her to listen and be able to contain this knowledge. I carried on: "Yes, the penis is a rod of light that aims to nourish with love, with the infinite light of the creation, with attention, with the desire to give and receive, in communication with the woman he is with. [14]The male energy comes to remind us, inspire us, and illuminate the darkness and ignorance, to fill us with love and to raise the level of awareness."

I stopped for a moment and turned to Beth: "Do you get what I mean?"

"In theory, yes," she answered. "I think I have never experienced that, but it's ok, I have something to aspire to! Can you please answer my question earlier about relaxing when the man comes inside me?"

"To receive the gift of male sperm inside you is to receive the purest spark of the Creator. The seed of creation and existence is in the sperm. When the sperm enters our bodies, breathe and agree to receive inside you the masculine knowledge that is encoded within it. It gives you power and more wisdom on how to work

14. The root of male in Hebrew, 'zachar,' is the three letters z, c, and r. The male calls to mind, 'lehazcir,' which shares the same three-letter root of z, c, and r.

and conduct your male energy. Afterwards, the penis really is physically limp and, if you have a released and freed vagina that hasn't experienced deprivation during the act of love, your vagina will be able to continue to get pleasure and accept the change of the penis that was in a rigid state and brought one kind of pleasure, to pleasure of a different kind."

I looked at Beth to make sure with a glance that she understood what I was talking about, if not from her head, then from her heart. I felt her body had relaxed and she was able to absorb some of what I said.

"There are more ways to experience pleasure from a relaxed, freed penis," I said. "In a situation where the man has passed the peak of his pleasure, he has raised his energy upwards to his heart. And then, his penis is still hard, but softer and that softness is also very pleasurable both to a woman and to a man."

Ember caught my eye and said: "How beautiful to hear you put this into words. I wish I had the wisdom to internalize this. First, let me find a steady partner with whom I can release and fully let go and not be occupied with the idea that he could leave any moment and that I will never see him again. All this casual sexuality is tiring me out. I want to be in a relationship, to have a genuine partner and say yes to this path."

I looked at her lovingly while saying a silent prayer that she receives what she seeks and finds a steady partnership. And that until then, she would be able to enjoy this from the present moment and from the sexual encounters that come into her life.

"I know that feeling," I answered. "Even when a man comes in a woman lovingly, her vagina—for all different reasons—sometimes clenches up and contracts. Do you know when everything is totally in place and you really wanted him to just enter you already, but then something closes?"

Carol answered: "I know it, yes, and when a man touches me in a way that wasn't exactly what my body wanted. In that moment, all my desire fades away."

"Most of the time, I continued even when I didn't feel like it," said Iris.

"And that's a good example of how we create the contractions in our vagina due to not listening to our inner selves," I said. "And then the vagina starts to talk, or sometimes develops fungus infections to wake us up."

The sun began to hide between the clouds and the sky turned gray once again. Noa got up and added three logs to the fire. She sat close to the fireplace, a little outside of the intimate circle we had created. I let her take that space from the group so she would be able to feel herself.

"Why is it so hard for us to be the container, the receptacle that contains the light?" I asked the group.

"First of all," Ruth answered, "the man doesn't always put in light. He doesn't always have that conscious awareness. Many men have no idea that is their role: to bring down light into the woman's vagina. They need to be reminded of that!"

"That is true, but right now let's start from a point where the man does want to bring love to the woman he is with," I said. "What prevents us from containing light and love?"

"Even if a really sweet man will come to me full of good intentions," said Ember, "if he enters me without asking me permission—with words, with a look or with a touch, it will surely cause my vagina to contract and won't allow me to contain anything afterwards."

"To get permission is really new to me—what? Just before the penetration itself?" asked Iris.

Ember nodded and Iris said, as if speaking to herself, "I will try to speak about that with my husband. I hope he will understand why I'm even asking that of him."

"I suggest, in any case, that you converse with him about it only when you understand within yourself the importance and meaning of that for yourself," I offered. "When that is clear to

178

you, it will raise the likelihood of him understanding what you are talking about."

I looked at the women and asked: "Are there any other reasons?"

"There are. When people don't listen to me until the end or from the infinite history of tension between men and women," said Carol. "From the times I don't consent and it's hard for me to get pleasure, I tense up from fear of being hurt, from the belief I am not worthy of love, fear of rape; from the tension that penetrates inside me or from the tension that movement and pace of life creates inside me; from the shopping; from the overdraft in the bank; from taking care of the children. We have an endless list of reasons. In the end, it's to know how to let go, to leave the noise on the side and surrender."

"Imagine to yourselves how much pleasure and expansion is possible from the experience of a man penetrating you out of a genuine desire and intention to nourish you," I said. "What abundance of gifts and prosperity will come to you? It's important for me to emphasize the gates of pleasure also open the gates of pain and they sit on the same continuum That means for most women, the vagina bears not only personal, but collective pain. Sometimes, the pleasure will overwhelm the pain. With a present penis, it is possible to heal that pain. We are asked to breathe into the pain, to listen, to let go, and to dissolve the pain, so that we allow more male energy to connect inside us, to merge with us and to illuminate our hearts. A man who comes from love and knows his purpose can penetrate a woman with the intention to heal, even to the point of soothing a hurt shoulder, a cramped muscle, an aching heart. He can bring to the woman goodness and great medicine. Sometimes, as part of the healing process, pain, sadness, and tears seek to arise, to cleanse oneself and to let go," I said as I looked at them.

Ellie asked: "Does it really influence us up to the level of release of bodily pains?"

"I'd be interested in hearing what my medical colleagues at the hospital have to say about that," said Ruth.

"If you have the bravery to talk to them about that," I answered, "some of them will think you're talking nonsense and others will be interested and ask you where you learned such things, or what can be done to make that happen."

Ruth smiled: "Chances are I won't say a word about it at the hospital. Maybe in the end, I'll have a new relationship with some doctor and then I'll have to tell him about it because I'm pretty sure he'll have no clue!"

"You are the messengers to the men you meet," I said. I concluded with, "You are the ones who set boundaries; you are the ones who agree to be the receptacle to contain love. Pass on the message to the men in your lives, to your sons. Explain to men to stop getting confused from the sexual power that flows through them and to learn to use it exactly in the manner that brings love and the light of love to the world."

I took a deep breath. I looked outside through the window and saw a spider on a tree branch. It was reminiscent of the power that is hidden in the web of life that we weave. I said a silent prayer in my heart for a powerful feminine network that would write, in new letters, the language of sexuality on the Earth; and the network of men and women who choose the way of the heart and leave their mark for generations to come.

"Growth is needed on both parts. This includes the deepening of your agreement to be a receptacle, a womb that is devoted to receiving nourishment and inner observation. From this comes the recollection of the divine, of all creation, of the cosmic meeting between masculine and feminine creating a sacred space of love and holiness together." I took a deep breath and carried on: "In a few hours, we will part ways. I marvel at the beauty of each one of you and from witnessing the layers start to peel away. I know that sexual healing is a life-long journey. I am happy for every single woman who embarks upon this journey. Part of releasing, relaxing, and empowering the vulva comes from the expression in our meeting with the masculine energy.

"The essence of the male energy is different from that of the female one. Let us respect that. When we live in dignity with both these forces that together form the whole, a sexual union will take on a different form. When the vagina agrees to be nourished, she is released; she can let go. When the penis agrees to give nourishment, the vagina can be liberated—and so, too, the penis is content to give It's a mutual, reciprocal process. I feel we need a short respite. Let's go outside for a ten-minute break, prepare a cup of tea, and snack on something small."

"Yes, that's very fitting right now," said Ember as she got up. She prepared a cup of tea for Beth and Ruth, and then one for herself, and went outside. I felt as though my entire body was awake in vitality from the facilitation of the workshop and from the fascinating subject of balance between the male and female.

The discourse over male energy from a place of understanding and responsibility from the female energy was important. It's very easy to blame the man next to me, instead of taking responsibility for my personal actions. When I take responsibility and make changes, it resonates within my relationship. In any case, I know how much mental power is needed to leave these patterns of guilt and criticism behind.

I took a deep breath to sense from inside how I felt and what my situation was. I went to the toilet and when I walked, out I made myself a cup of verbena tea and sat back down in my place.

Ruth approached me and said: "I really want to say thank you to you. This workshop has awakened in me something new in my understanding of the separation from my husband; that it was necessary to wake me up."

"I am happy to hear that," I said to her and gave her a hug. "I have a feeling this knowledge that is coming to you is going to take you a long way and will change the way that you treat yourself, the way you encounter the world, and, specifically, your relations with men." I looked at her eyes and carried on: "You are so amazing and worthy, with a deep wisdom that helps others so much. You are an ophthalmologist; you know eyes are the window to the soul. Through them you can see to great depths, and you are able. Agree to use them. Give your gift."

Ruth looked at me, amazed: "You've got me. I never dare tell people what I see."

"Please, dare," I asked her. "Use your ability wisely, but I am sure you will help many people that you meet in the hospital. Who knows what other channels it will open for you when you dare to say more about what you see with confidence and ease." She smiled at me gratefully and went outside.

*I choose to have in my life nourishing and loving male energy. Thank you!*

*I choose here and now to activate the coils of my DNA in all the worlds, times, dimensions, and layers for a life in love, dignity, and self-appreciation. I recognize myself fully as being worthy of love and life—life that penetrates me only with honor, attentiveness, and love.*

# THE ESSENCE OF FEMININE ENERGY

Most of the women went outside to bask in the gentle winter sun. I took a moment for myself while in the workshop space. I lifted my head and saw the oak tree that I love so much. Just by looking at it, I feel so inspired and receive a tremendous boost of energy. I closed my eyes, resting my hand on my vaginal area, breathing and listening to what she was whispering to me. I called on the group's collective female vulva to understand what is needed to continue. I envisioned a statue of a beautiful goddess with a wide pelvis and large breasts. Her eyes were human, compassionate, and bore into mine, smiling softly at me with tenderness, humility, and love. I felt the essence of the divine goddess sitting down across from me, asking me to celebrate womanhood and femininity.

I recollected the infinite feminine powers associated with the creation of life and creation itself, which are available to women by virtue of being women. That was the vision that appeared to me and felt so very much alive. I understood the message: to deepen our understanding and experience of the feminine energy.

After ten minutes or so passed, I called the women back to the room. I felt the sun outside was keeping them from coming back in. I went out and at that moment felt, too, just how wonderful it was outside. I went to bring a mat, putting it out on the deck, the green grass glistening in the sun and full of life. "We will sit here," I declared, "and then go out for our afternoon break."

"Wonderful idea," said Iris. "Maybe I'll go and bring some pillows?" She brought out eight pillows from under the nylon and spread them out in a circle. We all sat. Everyone was happy from the refreshing change of scenery and even I was satisfied by my ability to be in tune with the moment.

I looked at the women, smiled, and said: "How amazing! We are continuing and diving now into more layers and depths of the feminine energy. It's simply perfect, I think, that we are speaking about this while sitting outside! The essence of the feminine energy is the Earth. When I am connected to Mother Earth, it's easier for my vagina to let go." I saw Beth's surprised look. I felt she wanted to say something, but she didn't say a thing. Her look changed and her face softened. I was happy to see that. I said a prayer to myself for the connection to the Earth and said: "Put your hands on the ground. Yes, it's still a little cold and wet, but it's still pleasant to touch."

Some of them got down from the deck and others needed to change their seats to be in a comfortable place, but everyone organized themselves and placed their palms on the earth.

"As part of the agreement to release and empower the vulva," I carried on, "it's important to connect with and deepen the connection to Mother Earth, with her spirit and energy. Feel her; be her. We say: 'From dust you came and to dust you return.' Every cell in our bodies is made from minerals and substances that came from the Earth. The Earth is you, me, and every one of us."

It was quiet. We could hear the wind, the chirping of the birds, and feel the frequency of the Earth reverberate inwards. Just by sitting on the ground, Mother Earth implicitly conveys the deep connection she has with every woman.

I began to hum deep, low tones. I stopped for a moment and asked: "I invite you all to release the sound of the Earth that comes through you. Focus on the low tones. We, as women, are in essence a tool that allows the Earth to create and to create life, through the sacred womb that dwells within us. Come, let's sing with our wombs together and create the oeuvre that seeks to be born through us together in this moment."

No words can describe the magic that came after that. A river of tones in gibberish arose, perhaps a little like Native American songs, in a powerful volume that shakes entire worlds. Ember sang in her full power. She affected Beth, who sang and danced. Noa, who until now had a fairly quiet voice, sang at the top of her lungs. There was a moving harmony between us all. We sang like that for about ten minutes.

Little by little, I lowered my voice until I went quiet. The women gave in to the beat that I brought and there was stillness. After a few moments of healing silence, I said: "Rest your palm of your hands on your wombs. Breathe into her, speak to her, ask her what she requires from you so that you may connect to the Earth that you embody."

Ember answered: "I am receiving the word listen."

Noa said: "To walk barefoot."

"I see some kind of vision. I am walking in the hills of Jerusalem, hugging the trees," said Ruth and laughed.

Ellie carried on: "To go out into nature and notice the animals I meet; the caterpillar, the dog, the fly. They are coming to bring me a message."

"To cultivate my garden, to do it myself, not to just let my gardener do it all," said Beth.

I added: "To go and dip into the springs, into water sources that emanate from the Earth."

"I see a lot of different types of earth: sand, limestone, hard rock, fertile soil, and a request to connect to the various variations and qualities of ground," Carol finished the round.

The sun continued to shine on us, keeping us warm. I opened my eyes for a moment and saw a bird of prey flying high in the skies, reminding me of the ability to look at the bigger picture and identify the possibilities, to catch exactly what I want with sharp, focused vision.

I smiled in gratitude to the bird that supported the workshop space and said: "Speak with the parts of the Earth in your bodies, that bleed into the earth. Walk barefoot on the Earth, speak to her, listen to her voice, lie down on her, merge with her, and seek her support. The Earth charges us, grounds us, shakes and rattles us from inside like the tremor of an earthquake. She is steady, resilient, omniscient. Mother Earth is a living, breathing being, part of the eternal divinity of the infinite unity of creation. Agree deep inside yourselves to connect with more of the source that supports your lives. The vagina and the womb are like a cave that dwells in the heart and core of the Earth," I said as I put in a request for the help of the great mother to give me the words to demonstrate more of the power in the direct bond between each woman and the fertile soil that she is. "The vaginal canal is like a tunnel, a cavity, and from her springs the unique creation that we are. Through her, life is born. When the seed of life comes inside her, the fertile soil nourishes and charges the seed with more life. The fusion of the male and female, between the seed of life and egg of love, occurs in your body. You are fertile earth."

I stopped for a moment and breathed. I felt that I was becoming the mouth of mother earth. I asked for more strength so that I may be able to contain the power that was passing through me, and carried on: "When you give birth, you are a wild, knowing, and powerful, lioness. The ground trembles and you tremble with her. You open up into a tremendous life force that bursts through you. You envelop and caress like soft sand, in a released, relaxed, expanding vagina, and allow the spring of life that emanates from within you!"

"The more that you deepen your connection with the earth that you are, and the more you will get to know her and respect her, the easier it will be to give birth. Be both fed and nourished at the same time."

I stopped the flow of words, took a deep breath, and everyone took a deep breath spontaneously, too. I said: "Repeat after me: I choose and I live in communication and connection with the earth that I am."

They repeated after me and I continued: "Feel, sense, imagine or think that from your naval there is an umbilical cord that connects to the core of the earth and always nourishes you. Be with that a moment."

Suddenly I heard rustling in the grass next to me. I was amazed to see a turtle. That had never happened to me in this space before. I continued on in gratitude for the support of the universe: "I am open to the channel of nourishment of the universe," I said, "and to all creation, thank you, thank you, thank you."

They repeated after me: "I am open to the channel of nourishment of the universe," I joined in with them and raised my voice. They rode the wave and brought more power to their own voices. I smiled and sat down. I felt that the turtle was a private message just for me and didn't share her presence with the others. I knew that if she wanted everyone to see her, she would move, take a step further, and someone would spot her.

Everyone sat down. Ember lay on her back and sighed deeply. Noa lay on her stomach and let her body recharge. I let the grace of that connection be, each one taking it in their own way. I love the feeling of that connection so very much. Hallelujah!

"Thank you for that moment and the special grace that was created for us from that connection. Let's all sit up," I said. It took a few moments until everyone collected themselves and returned to sitting.

"It's so much fun to feel that special connection inside, through awareness of the earth," said Ember.

"Breathe that special feeling inwards," I requested. "I hope that what you have gone through will continue to be with you throughout your lives."

"I have a question," said Noa with a little apprehension. "Sorry, maybe you've already explained it, but I don't fully understand the connection between releasing, relaxing, and empowering the vulva with the connection to the earth. Can you explain it again please?" her blue eyes met mine.

"Thank you for the question," I said and answered her. "The vulva is the ground of the body and is situated in a similar location. The head is the sky, and when seated, the vulva is closest to the ground and parallel to it. Perhaps that is why the bottom of the pelvis is called the base, because it grounds our bodies. The vagina receives sperm inside her; so too the earth receives seeds. The vulva flourishes and the earth flourishes. In ancient times, caves were thought to be sacred and were thought to be the divine vulva that gave birth to the world.

When the pelvic area is released of tension and the vagina is relaxed, with no stopper that blocks the opening of the canal, the energy of earthy wisdom can reach and enter into the body through the soles of the feet, to fill the hips and the vagina. When we are full of life energy we feel the desire to create, and we want to reproduce life on earth. When we have a connection and are in communication with the earth — the vulva, the opening and the womb can be more relaxed. And why? Because we are in touch and connected to our primal innate nature as women. By accepting the female parts of us, we create more inner integrity, more serenity, and we learn to work with the whole energy reserve. More power is available to us."

"Thank you, now it's clearer to me," said Noa.

"What else do you think helps in relation to womanhood and femininity that we should pay attention to?" I asked them.

"One of the things that makes me stressed during sex is the fear that I will get pregnant," said Carol. "I had the IUD for years, but I realized that it detached me from my femininity. I stopped using the device, but my vagina still won't let go."

"That's an important point," I answered. "When you know your body, your rhythm and you trust it, your vagina can let go. Most of us were not taught to trust our intuition and listen to the quintessential signs our body shows us our cycles. Some contraceptives prevent us from this natural ability. The way back to creating trust in our personal rhythm is through honest and authentic listening. It's on us to trust ourselves, and so too to learn to listen to our personal fertility rhythms. And if you still choose to use contraceptives, ask for forgiveness from your body. In any case continue to learn, to identify which contraceptive method is right for you to use depending on the stage you are in during your personal cycle."

"What do you mean?" asked Ellie.

"I mean for each person's moon time," I answered her. "There is a time when the moon is full, that is to say — when she is in the peak of ovulation. The new moon time is the time of the menses: the blood time, when the moon is born, is when the body wakes to a new movement to prepare to absorb the sperm. There is a whole life cycle here of filling up and emptying once a month.

That's the rhythm that each one of us is influenced by. It's about time that we start to connect with and relate to our personal rhythms with respect. Rest during the days of menstruation and run with the wind in the days of your ovulation. That's the movement that takes place inside of us at all times!"

"But what should I do if, on the day of my period, I have meetings?" Ruth asked.

"If you really cannot cancel," I replied, "speak with your body, and let it know that you know you are bleeding right now. Don't be hard on yourselves and find a way to relax into it. If you know when you are due for your monthly bleed, it's worthwhile not to commit to too much. The cycle is not a time of the blood but rather our monthly cycle as a whole. The menstruation is the time of blood, and therefore we can say that we've gotten our period, but not our cycle." I love talking about menstruation and about our personal connection created with blood and how it influences the entirety of our lives as women. I felt the grace that was in the fact that we were sitting outside, in the heart of the fresh green that marked the beginning of winter.

I continued: "It's important to me that we understand something fundamental in the context of our awareness of the

189

body and our relationship with it. We were born into a patriarchal society that especially admires and values the masculine movements in the world. The social codes give less respect and inclusion of the female movement, which is slower and more patient. There is endless critique about how a woman's body should look. There is endless preoccupation with weight gain and loss. Most advertisements show young and shapely women. That is the code for what is thought to be beautiful in our society. This has all been inherited over hundreds of years and has made it so that we don't know our own bodies, or the movement of our cycles, or the movement of our moon. This shows a lack of love and deep appreciation for when our blood arrives and its deep gifts that goes beyond bringing children into the world. There is practically no love for the secretions and fluids that pass through our vaginas or recognition of their significance and importance for health."

"For a few years now, I have used a natural method of contraception, and it's wonderful," said Ember. "Thanks to that method, I got to know my body. I know exactly when I am ovulating and when I have no chance of getting pregnant. I pay attention to my fluids that pass through my body because they reflect my fertility situation."

"I too learned this," I said and carried on: "After a full year of failing to get pregnant, I learned to understand my rhythm in more depth and to identify when I am fertile and I did get pregnant."

"So, what you are saying basically is that a woman has the ability to know exactly when she is ovulating and when she is not fertile?" asked Ruth.

"Yes," I answered, "and she can get to a level where she chooses and knows exactly when she will get pregnant. Unfortunately, it's still not passed from mother to daughter. Please go to a course and learn in depth about listening carefully to the signs of your own bodies," I said as I looked at each one of the women. "Most of us were taught not to trust ourselves," I carried on, "and were encouraged to take the pill to prevent pregnancy or put in the IUD."

Iris looked at me and asked to speak: "My vagina is not at all released, but when I gave birth, I felt that I knew how to be in labor and that I was asked to trust this. But really, I had to be allowed to be alone and able to get through this challenging thing."

"I think that I understand something," said Ellie. "Essentially, the more you resist the body, criticize it, hate the blood and ignore your natural cycles, the more the body will signal and create more tension."

Ruth continued passionately: "If that's the case, it's so clear why so many women have extreme premenstrual symptoms (PMS). We live in a society that is ashamed and hides everything to do with menstruation. It causes us to contract and creates pains in the body. I pray to the Creator of the world... May good medicine come to women in the world. May we love ourselves!" she said with her hands on her heart.

Ellie carried on: "And basically, if I love my blood with the intention, then my vulva can let go more."

"So, the menstruation is actually a gift. This is really revolutionary for me, I have to say," said Noa.

"Once a month we are given the gift of blood," I said. "It's a gateway to power, giving us the power to create life and bring children. What else can menstruation give us?"

"Connection to our inner cyclical movement," said Ember. "When I live with other women, we get our periods together. There is some kind of hidden energy that flows between women."

I had to relate to that and so I said: "Me too. When I was a teenager, I always got my period at the same time as my mother and sister. It's the sisterhood! By the way, that is something else that helps us release the vagina. A female group — sisters of the heart — is very important for feminine health. Isn't it so much fun for us to sit together, as women, and talk about sexuality and femininity?"

"The menstruation reminds me of life but also of death," said Beth, "because the womb cries a little every month anew because it hasn't succeeded in getting pregnant."

Ellie added: "Every month we change seasons of a whole year. It's crazy to think about that — winter, spring, summer, autumn."

I nodded in agreement and felt in my heart the happiness that this understanding was permeating the women.

"My personal cycle connects me to the cycle of the universe," said Ruth, "deepening the recognition and awareness of the fact that we are part of the wonder and exciting part of all creation. We are actually creators ourselves. The spirit of g-d passes through our wombs in order to bring children to the world."

Iris looked at me and asked: "How do you suggest we use our menstrual time?"

I answered her and everyone: "I invite you to practice experiencing joy when your blood comes. Encourage the women around you to rejoice, too. During the days of your menstruation, you are invited to ride the wave of the cleansing that your body undergoes and identify what else inside you desires to be cleansed and released with the blood. Take time for yourself to rest. The blood should not hurt. It asks you to rest the body and soul. Collect the blood, water the garden with it, use it in a ritual that you perform around the fire if you can, and empty the blood directly into the ground. The more that women connect to their blood, the more healing power will mix with the earth and increase the chances for world peace. The more that we women return our blood to the earth, the more we free and release the earth from the need for blood from those killed in war.[15] It reminds us of the direct ties between them. I invite us all to bring our daughters to an empowering meeting with their blood."

---

15. Within the Hebrew word for earth, 'adama,' there is the word for blood, 'dam.'

"What luck that I am finished with all this menstruation," said Beth, "it was a burden on me for most of my years and I wouldn't have been able to change my perception."

I smiled at her. "You never know. The fact that you're here at all means you are already releasing and empowering your vulva. Maybe you will have a conversation with your grandchild and give her the perspective that opens a new direction for her. That is already a very blessed thing!"

Ellie added: "I bet I'm your granddaughter's age, so we have closed the circle," she looked at Beth and smiled.

"So when I respect the blood that I had or basically respect the fact that I don't have blood," said Beth, "it means that my vulva is relaxed and empowered? Because the hatred of blood contracts the vagina?"

I nodded in agreement with her words. The winter sun was so pleasant. I looked sideways and saw a shimmering raindrop, shining on a leaf. The encounter between light, water, plants, and earth always aroused wonder within me. "Alright ladies, hands on the womb for a moment," I requested, and everyone placed their hands on their lower stomachs.

"Let's thank our wombs for being a direct channel to creation," I continued, "and for the privilege that we have for living in cycles. Whoever has finished their menstruation — you are invited to be in gratitude for the privilege to be an open channel to ancient wisdom of the feminine. And add: I love and I learn about the flow of my vagina fluids! For all the variations, she supports me and guides me."

I let everyone utter their intentions silently to themselves and after a few moments I added: "Fluids are situated in our vaginal canal at all times of the month and they are our signal. The fluids clean our openings and therefore, I don't recommend using soap because it throws the whole area out of balance. Our vaginas know how to clean themselves; trust them!"

Noa's face lit up: "I feel that you are raising issues here that call for me to make a big change. Life has already shown me that

I have the ability to change. I hope that I find the strength of faith and perseverance to shed my skin and that I will be able to live a life from a place of listening to my cycles, my blood, and my inner rhythms."

I smiled with pleasure. I knew deep inside that from her very speech something had already deepened in her inner listening.

"I wish for all of you to achieve this," I said. "Step by step this will bring us to life in connection to our personal-feminine rhythms."

I inhaled a deep breath and closed my eyes in inner contemplation for the next piece of knowledge that may seek to come into the circle. A pleasant silence filled the space. An image of a man and woman hugging and melting into soft and pleasant love flashed in front of my eyes, and I understood. The next subject will be connected to the male and the female, and the gift that their togetherness and partnership brings to the world. I breathed another deep breath and asked for the support of the universe to convey this knowledge to the light.

*I choose life in connection to the wisdom of the earth and my unique cyclical rhythm. I remember that I deserve a life of connection. I deserve a life of pleasure! Thank you!*

# SACREDNESS, LISTENING, PLEASURE, AND MY QUEENDOM

"This morning, we spoke about the essence of male energy that penetrates love into the world, as well as the female energy essence that is a receptacle for love from the world. I want to talk about the meeting between the two when their unification creates a celebration of love and life in so many ways and layers," I said.

"What you describe sounds utopian, but one time I sat with my friend and she mentioned a concept that I never really understood. She called it sacred sexuality. Maybe that's what you're talking about?" Asked Iris. She breathed out loudly and carried on: "Can you explain what that has to do with releasing, relaxing, and empowering the vulva?"

I was happy to hear her question and I opened it up to the floor.

"My answer would be no," said Ruth. "From how I understand it, sacred sexuality sanctifies the act of love from the recognition of the opportunity to experience unity and deep divinity."

Ember chimed in: "I think that it refers to the space where the divine feminine meets the divine masculine and merges as one in infinite cosmic unity."

"[16] Like an almond blossom bursting with beauty out of hibernation, bringing so much light and joy, the sacred requires us

---

16. In Hebrew, the word for holy, 'kadosh,' contains the word for almond, 'shaked.'

to be determined and persevere in our devotion to the unknown. Its fruit is an abundance of life force, connection to the source, happiness, and power."

"How is that related to an empowered vulva?" asked Ellie.

"An empowered vulva supports the creation of a reality of sacred sexuality," I said. "Part of the sacred essence is when the penis penetrates the vagina in love. The penis remembers the essence of his role, which is to illuminate the holy container. A relaxed and empowered vulva can contain love. It is very hard to contain love in a contracted vagina. A man can remind the woman and the vagina to let go. What's important is that a dialogue is formed over what is happening inside of her. An attentive discourse allows for more relaxation. The vagina can clearly communicate its wishes as it activates its senses, connects to the womb, and links with a direct line to the secrets of creation. The vagina speaks to us, feels, signals, knows, and chatters in her own language. Sexuality with sacredness helps us listen to whatever the vagina wants to tell us."

Iris entered the conversation and said: "I don't understand."

"Try practicing the act of listening to your vulva," I answered, "breathing into her helps to deepen the act of listening. Take five minutes every day and breathe into her, paying attention to what happens to her and how your listening ability to your vaginal senses develops."

"What a concept: vagina senses and having the vagina sense!" Beth said smiling, before her face suddenly fell. "I've never truly let my vagina feel anything. I avoided her. Basically, I avoided myself, but perhaps it's because I became dry. I began to listen to her and something new was able to come through. In truth, I do want to keep having sex and finally I have a partner to do it with."

"I truly wish for this change to happen for you," I said. "The call is to take responsibility for removing limiting beliefs around sexuality and the life force operating inside of us, and have faith in our ability to create change. Also, practice the exercises that we already did together and rekindle the return of your life fluids."

Beth listened to my words, took a deep breath, and said: "Thank you, I'm going to try that. I pray that change will come!"

Ember smiled and said to her: "Believe in it!"

A moment of silence fell. Ellie turned to me and said: "Can you go back and elaborate on your explanation of sacred sexuality?"

"It's hard to explain sacred sexuality in words," I said. "It involves magic, wonder, presence, listening, creation of love, softness, wildness, happiness, breath, agreement to give, and agreement to receive. Each time is different of course. These characteristics are found in sacred love-making." I took a deep breath and carried on: "There is a grace that is created during love-making when the divine within us merges with the great and cosmic divine. There is understanding that is deeply and clearly experienced in the pleasure of the encounter between the male and female. Love-making becomes a process that enables development and growth."

I asked for help from my guide because I knew deep down that sacred sexuality is very personal and is experienced differently from person to person. I felt that there was more information that wanted to come through me, and I let the words flow out of me. I said: "Put one hand on your heart and the other on your vaginal area. Let's connect the two. We are going to make a prayer for a beneficial and positive connection between the sexual beings that we are and our soft, sensitive hearts. I invite each one of you to place your own intention and desire from sacred sexuality. You are invited to add: "I choose, practice and explore sacred sexuality in my daily life. This knowledge is available to me. Thank you, thank you, thank you!"

I felt the frequency shift. I relaxed and felt grateful for the perfect expression that came to me. The sun began to hide between the clouds. I felt that it was about time to go back inside the yurt. Our afternoon break was nearly upon us and we would soon be closing the workshop. Sometimes I would feel the time was too short. This is knowledge that takes time to digest. But having an overload of information is also not supportive to the process.

As if she had heard my thoughts, Ellie piped up: "It's a little cold, maybe we should go back inside?"

"Yes," I answered, and everyone got up and went inside.

*I choose to practice and devote myself to sacred sexuality. This knowledge is available to me. Every cell in my body is awakened and vibrates sacred sexuality. This happens in all my worlds, times, dimensions, and layers.*

We sat back down in a circle in the womb-like and warm yurt. "I already sense the end of our workshop," I said. "It's all at once challenging and freeing when I start to prepare us for the end," I said with a smile and carried on: "Why else should we relax and empower our vulvas?" I asked.

"Maybe when the vagina is empowered and relaxed, we find goodbyes endings easier," said Ember with a half-smile.

"If I am in a sexual encounter and my partner immediately gets up and leaves," said Noa, "my vagina will constrict entirely."

"Correct," I answered, "that's exactly why there are steps to take ahead of the end. When love-making is over we stay together in bed, hugging, and then slowly each one can feel their own body and leave. Only after that, each person goes their own way. At some point, your kingdom becomes second nature and, at her base level, your vagina is empowered, released, relaxed, and content, knowing what she wants. When you listen to her, she can be your compass. When you let go, you remember that you are worthy," I said.

"I suffer from so many fungal infections in my vagina," said Iris. "I've taken medications, changed my diet, and still, the infections come back. If my vagina is my compass, where is she directing me?" asked Iris.

"The fungus is a compass. It is the vagina's way of talking to us," I said. "The vagina calls on us to listen and pay attention to what she is trying to tell us. She is putting up a clear boundary to observe, learn, and be more precise with your movements towards yourself, your sexuality, and the world. Learning to be in communication with your vagina involves listening to her signaling to you. It is part of the ability to relax, because full attentive listening exists from an internally relaxed space — a space of inner peace and presence. When we are in communication and pay attention to our vulva, chances are that the infections in the vagina will go and lessen. They could even disappear, appearing occasionally when we forget to be in communication or when the vagina wants to signal something to us that we simply haven't noticed... When we are in communication with the vagina, we are powerful and healthier.

"When we have an inner determination to truly love and respect ourselves and experience from the knowledge that we are worthy of love, it is fitting that only a man of love will enter into our space. When we deserve pleasure, our ability to relax the vagina deepens and our vaginal sensors become more sophisticated. When the 'no' comes up, it's obvious, and the same goes for the 'yes.' The body signals and we pay attention to it."

"I have to add something," said Ember in a voice full of life. "It's not only that we are worthy, but also that we know in our entire bodies that we are queens!" A big smile crept upon her face.

"Why don't you give us a description of a queen. What does that mean for you?" I asked her.

"When I am a queen, I am first and foremost worthy, and all the world is in service to me," Amber replied. "I know that I am worthy of a life in pleasure. I experience myself sexually with comfort, ease, and joy."

"For me," began Noa, speaking clearly and with confidence, "it's a deep and profound knowing that I am wonderful" she spoke, and her words left a trail of magic dust behind.

"You are truly wonderful," Amber said as she smiled at Noa. "Why did it take you such a long time to realize that?!" Amber said, looking straight at her. Noa smiled.

"When a woman is a queen," Amber added, elaborating on the concept. "She knows that she deserves a man who penetrates her and connects to her only with pure love. She is a queen that lives her inner experience. Everything she wants to happen actually happens."

"Let's connect our Queendom and our sexuality," I suggested and carried on at the sight of the nodding in front of me: "When a woman is relaxed, she lives in her own power. It's a looseness that comes with presence and calmness. As I already mentioned, the yoni feels everything. Information enters and exits the yoni all the time."

I looked at them to check that they understood me and continued to speak in a clear and confidant voice: "When we are attentive to our vulva and we pay attention to how she feels, we remain with an open and courageous heart and face what the vulva feels. We agree to live in power. A life of power is a life in majesty. So, what do you all say?! Do you agree to empower and relax your vulvas?" I said and looked into the beautiful eyes of each one of the participants.

My eyes came upon Ellie and she said: "And what if my vulva experiences attraction to a married man? What do I do with that? Is that power too?"

"Let's start from the fact that we are allowed to flow the energy of pleasure in our bodies," I replied.

"Our animalistic instincts and sexual energy can be aroused by a beautiful flower, a baby breastfeeding, a handsome man, and a beautiful woman, all while guiding a workshop, experiencing a significant moment and many other things that simply flow the life energy within us. After our afternoon break, we will talk about how to flow this sexual energy with awareness through our body and experience pleasure from the beauty the world has to offer, regardless of the choice to mingle physically or sexually with someone else."

Ellie related to my words: "Basically what you're saying is that all energy of pleasure or, for the purpose of this conversation, sexual energy that I experience in my body, is permissible, and that I am allowed to experience pleasure from it regardless of the situation from which it arises?"

"Yes, that's exactly it," I answered. "We learn to manage and direct the energy with wisdom and respect for ourselves and those around us. We agree to feel it in our bodies, ride the wave of our sexual energy, enjoy it, and channel it as a life energy that supports us in creating our unique fulfillment in the world. This brings us to the topic that we will talk about after the break. It is the topic with which we will close the workshop: How to ride the wave of sexual energy and enjoy the frequency for strengthening the creation of reality in our everyday lives."

I looked at them and opened all of my senses in order to sense whether or not everyone was on my wavelength. It can be a very sensitive and delicate subject, because most people were never taught about pleasure or how sexual energy flows through the body. I felt it was important for the participants to understand that they are allowed to feel pleasure in their bodies in a balanced way that supports them in conducting their day-to-day life. There were already wonderful smells of cooking coming from the kitchen, and the sun had come back to shine. I added: "I agree: a vulva that knows how to relax or contract its muscles supports us and of course supports the men during lovemaking. A released vulva can melt and plunge into infinite depths of love. A released vulva can be contracted and create endless waves of pleasure. I remind you that releasing and empowering the vulva is a choice of a life within our power. It's a unique journey for each person; there really is no one recipe."

I looked at the women, and I wanted to ensure that they understood everything I said so that a new light may shine through them. Their body language conveyed to me a strong "yes, we understand." But I also felt a question mark and some doubt, so I said: "I believe in you all! Let's take an hour and a half's break. We'll eat, rest, take a moment for ourselves, go outside, and form personal, private bonds with the earth."

*I remember and I choose to be worthy and attentive to my vulva. I live in pleasure and majesty.*

# RIDING THE WAVE

I felt I needed some quiet. I went to my bedroom and ate some fruit. I lay down on the bed and directed golden energy from my feet upwards through my body to the crown of my head. It always recharges me and helps me relax. I relaxed my face and let my body sink. I felt my mind drain of thoughts and my body soften and recharge between wakefulness and sleep. I felt a wave of powerful energy come through me as I breathed deeply and asked my guides to show me how to end the workshop in the most beneficial way for the participants.

I had not yet taught the next part of the workshop — creating reality by using sexual energy - and I had some hesitation. I asked for help in overcoming my fears. I prayed for the help of the creator as I fell into a short, sweet sleep. I awoke after half an hour, made tea, ate some fruit, and went outside feeling refreshed and renewed. Amber and Ruth were sitting outside together. Amber had a cigarette in hand, and it appeared as though they were deep in conversation. I smiled towards them and went over to the oak tree. I turned to face the tree trunk and hugged it, merging with it and asking it for a charge. I prayed for simple wisdom to flow through me and for clear and simple words to come to me. I love hugging trees. Many years ago, when I was 24 years old, I had a teacher who taught me to hug trees and merge with the tree. She taught me to be one with it, feel its deep roots,  the top of the tree merge with me, and enable the energy of the tree to balance me. A hug from a tree is a moment of sanity for me. It's grace, balance, and connection to the source.

When I felt ready to come back to the real world, I went to the kitchen to see if there was still some food left in the pans. I took some food and sat down to eat. Carol came by and asked to join me. "I still haven't eaten yet," she stated.

"Of course," I answered as she sat down opposite me. I looked at her and a wave of appreciation for her came over me. Her brown hair shone in the winter sunlight that came through the window into the kitchen.

"You know, it's not at all a given that I came here," said Carol. I smiled at her as she continued: "My initial encounter with sexual energy as a teenager was full of challenges and fear. For years I felt pretty frozen around the subject. I was as cold as ice. I had a friend who has since passed who always told me to deal with my issues regarding sexuality. Her death really rattled me and I realized that life is happening right now, and that if I don't take care of this issue stuck inside me, it will be too late. I went to therapy and slowly but surely something became unstuck. I am way more alive in my life. I do whatever I feel like doing, I'm free, and I feel more at ease now. It was very meaningful for me to make that change."

I looked at her softly and said: "Thank you for sharing that with me. I can say you've done wonderful work. I didn't feel that you were stuck, but rather the opposite: your openness and ability to connect is astounding." I gave her a hug.

"How lovely, it's so nice for me to hear that. It means I've gone on a journey," said Carol.

I finished eating, got up from the table, and put my plate in the sink before going back to the round and womb-like yurt. I looked out of the window. Mount Tavor could be seen today in all her glory. I requested from the wisdom of the goddess who dwells in the mountain to support me in the closing of the workshop. I lit sage and purified the space. I went to the fireplace and watched the fire before burning two more big logs of wood.

I listened to the whispers of the fire for a moment and then went to sit in my place on the cushions. I felt that the time had come for the circle to return. Beth arrived and sat next to me, giving me a hug. Her pleasant softness enveloping me. Everyone slowly trickled in and went to sit down in the circle, like a tribe of women sitting together.

"How are we all? I hope you enjoyed the food," I said, "and that you rested and gathered renewed energy. Part of releasing and empowering the vulva is the ability to rest with women and sisters, be together, bleed together, and experience life together. I suggest you all maintain a network of women in your lives. I suggest that you meet with them and have them as a support network." I smiled and ran my gaze over the women. I saw eyes full of clarity, tiredness, happiness, and curiosity.

I carried on: "Okay, let's get to the part that I am teaching for the first time. I am excited!"

Beth interrupted my speech and asked: "For the first time?!"

"Yes," I answered. "It's knowledge that came to me through my life experience. The core of it I learned from my own explorations in life and through gifts that I picked up from people I met along the way. The knowledge is tied to how we ride the wave of sexual energy and channel it into creative work or the reality of how we wish to live in our lives."

"I'm sorry, I don't understand what you're trying to say," said Ruth.

I smiled. "Don't worry, let's all take a deep breath, place a hand on our vaginal area, and be patient with the ability to absorb."

They rested their hands on their vaginal area and took a deep breath. "Wonderful! I invite you to open your senses and  listen to me from your vulvas, hearts, third eyes, and every place where your receptors are open. Are you with me?" I asked and they nodded in agreement. I continued: "Sexual energy is one of the strongest energy waves in the universe. It's a powerful wave. Can we all agree on this?" I looked at them and they nodded positively.

"Sexual energy is part of the sacred energy of the whole that we are. Since, at least for most of us, our sexual energy has been either partially or fully repressed and we haven't lived in peace with it, we have missed the opportunity to use it as a full charge of

205

energy to create the reality that we want in our lives. We have, in effect, cancelled our capacity to use our life forces fully."

"Wait, wait," Beth burst into the conversation, "are you trying to tell me that I can create reality with sexual energy? I don't understand. It can enable us to bring children, but how can it create an entire reality?!" she asked, with shock and anger.

"First of all — yes," I said, "I invite you to ride the sexual energy wave so that you can create reality and produce more support in your lives with that power. When we allow sexual energy to flow through us and we gladly welcome it, we can overcome fear by using that energy. This gives us a place for our full power that can generate everything. It can dismantle our most stuck structures, patterns, inner worlds, and the world at large, and lead to a new place. How do we do that? How do we ride that wave?" I paused for a moment, figuring out how I wanted to start.

"Let's start with something easy. Before you embark on a sexual encounter with yourselves or with a partner, place an intention. Tune in and request to dedicate this energetic wave to the fulfilment of something that you want. Think of it during this time. It would look like this: 'I am very happy and I choose ... to be present in my life.' The other option is for you to make the intention during your love-making. It can be with yourself or with a partner with or without his knowledge. Utter your intention in a whisper or out loud, however you like. If you're with a partner and you utter your intention out loud, it's nicer and more pleasant if he too will harness the intention. This creates a bigger wave and intensifies the reverberation of the intention. It is recommended that you also utter your intention while you orgasm. You're welcome to try. I used this during the time in my life when we were building our new house for the things that were stuck and delayed, and it worked wonders. Every time I remembered and hopped on the wave during the love-making, I placed an intention and the next day things that were on hold were released.

You are invited to play with it. Even if you aren't in a relationship or you're experiencing a less sexual period with your partner, you can ride that wave from your personal encounters when you are pleasuring yourselves."

Beth shifted uncomfortably and asked: "What do you mean, pleasure myself?" she took a deep breath and carried on. "You mean, to masturbate?"

"The word masturbation makes me cringe and straight away fills me with the feeling of hiding away with shame," I said. "The intention is the ability to pleasure yourselves without shame and feelings of guilt but rather with simplicity, confidence, delight, and joy. In addition, I suggest that you hop on the wave and channel the energy that runs through you to support the creation of your reality."

"That is great!" said Amber. "I've never thought about it this way. Thank you. I am going to try it straight away," she said, grinning.

"Wait," said Beth, "Not here — for the love of g-d!" she said, laughing.

"What other delicacies are you concocting for us? How else can we create reality through sexual energy?" asked Carol.

"It's possible to channel sexual energy beyond loving encounters," I said. "What I mean is that you can consciously choose to work with the sexual energy beyond sexual intercourse. It can be a sexual encounter with another person outside of a relationship, even if it just started a moment ago. A sexual encounter binds us as women to agree to be entered. But equally, we agree to give and penetrate with our energy for someone else. This is a connection of giving and receiving, or in other words: consent to enter the world and consent to let the world enter us. The same thing happens in our breathing patterns. When we inhale, we breathe in air and the world enters us. When we exhale, we let out air and enter the world."

I took a deep breath before continuing: "As long as we agree to empty out more air — to enter the world — we agree to more air and letting the world enter us. When we empty our lungs, we make space for more oxygen to enter the cavity; there is more space for more *prana* — life energy — to be present in our bodies. When I give generously and abundantly, I have more space inside of myself to receive broader support from the universe. Why am I talking so much about penetration? Because sexual relations include penetration and entry into chambers in our bodies and souls. For some people, it's easy to give to the world, but agreeing to let go and be in a position where they receive penetration — i.e. receiving from the world — brings up fears, restlessness, and an inability to let go." I stopped for a moment and looked at the women to check that they were following the information, which was new to most of them.

"Essentially, by agreeing to give and receive, we enter into a space where we want to live with the whole energy that we are We become inclusive of the sexual energy that we are, and enable the full flow of our electric current in every layer of our lives. We agree to give to enter the world and agree to receive to allow the world to enter us. Once one of these qualities becomes unbalanced, it challenges the notion of living our lives in presence and power with a high and vibrating conductivity. When we are at high intensity and conductivity, we experience sexual energy while we are in action and creating the world. When we have passion in our actions, chances are we experience sexual arousal, which is basically pleasure. The more that we accept this feeling, and consciously give that energy space by breathing it in and letting it flow easily in the body while riding the wave, the more we will discover joyful and vibrating energy available for creation and inspiration. If we close ourselves off, cringing away from sensations of pleasure that arise in our bodies, we are actually stopping the current of energy from moving freely in the body and recharging us in life. We consequently have less energy." I stopped for a moment, took a deep breath, and looked out the window. I saw winter sunbeams jutting out from the clouds, heading westwards, that reminded me that the end of the day was nearing. Long, luminous and beautiful sunbeams in orange-gold hue formed spectacular strips of light connecting the skies to the earth. I was moved by this beauty and afterwards I returned to look at the group.

"I have a question," said Amber. "I know that feeling you're talking about when it comes up. I've noticed that if a man is in my proximity while I'm experiencing that pleasure and power inside, I start to find him attractive and I want him."

I smiled. "Right, that's totally what happens. You can ride the wave and enter an intimate connection with that person. Another option is to consciously nourish yourself with this energy, and bestow it upon yourself in order to deepen your creativity. Become motivated with passion and sexual desire in a way that supports the realization of your dreams and increases movement from a place of passion and pleasure."

"Can you give a more concrete example?" asked Ruth.

"Yes. For example, when I play music with people, I sometimes feel sexual energy while I play. There's this experience of a deep merger with the melody and with whomever I am playing with. I have learnt to recognize it and allow the sexual energy to flow through me consciously, calmly and freely, and allow the melody to emanate from within me with an increased passion that gives me more inspiration, pleasure, and joy. But I could just as well experience arousal, want a sexual encounter, and roll with that. That's a choice; how to move and flow with my full energy sources so they support my creativity. Each time is different. I welcome you to try and practice it. It's a source that springs from your creative energy!"

I looked at them and recognized their looks of amazement and thrill. It made me so happy.

I took a deep breath and continued: "One of the ways to raise the entire wave frequency, including the sexual energy within us, is to have a real encounter with the world. Therefore, I want us to do an exercise in pairs. It's an exercise that really opens the heart and brings our hearts and bodies closer. Initially, do it with people close to you that you trust. We create a reality in which we are streaming a conscious wave and flow of giving and receiving. You'll see what happens."

This secret of energetic flow was given to me as a gift. I discovered it with my partner after I practiced it with him regularly. It's an exercise that I use in ceremonies that I facilitate, and yet I felt a desire, mixed with tension, to teach and transmit this knowledge. I lifted my head and looked out the window to the mountain, the oak tree, and the sun rays that penetrated through the clouds and created a wonderous beauty. I asked the bright light to support me. I know that living knowledge flows through me and I trust that the right words will come, even if I don't have any idea what the next word out of my mouth will be.

"Let's split into pairs," I requested, and the women sat opposite one another. Noa with Carol, Ruth with Iris, and Amber with Beth. I sat with Ellie.

Sit opposite one another and hold your hands in an eight; your right hand holds the right hand of your partner and your left holds their left hand so that the four palms are placed on top of each other. Here we have created a shape — the pattern of eight, with the palms of our hands as the center. We held hands and I continued on: "Close your eyes, relax your shoulders, your face, and your breath. Every time that we breathe air in, agree to receive and focus on your left hand. When we exhale, we agree to give and focus on our right hand. When we take in an inhalation we say: I agree to be penetrated and to connect. I receive. When we breathe out we say to ourselves: I agree to penetrate, I agree to give.

"Energetic flow and air pass consciously to the heart, and it's part of the flow of the eight pattern. Flow the energy from your left hand, through your heart center, to your right hand and from there to her right hand, her heart center her left hand, and back through your left hand. Breathe a few deep breaths and then, each one in their own time, open your eyes. I know that we aren't used to giving eye contact, but I really welcome you to stay there. Look deep inside the soul of the person in front of you. Agree to be present in your gaze from your infinite souls and into the infinite soul of the person in front of you. Devote yourself to the breath and the gaze and to a connection of hearts. Let the entire frequency that you are flow between you. You might start to feel pleasure in your body and a surge of powerful energy that is concentrated around your hands. I welcome you to agree to give everything to the wholeness that you are and cause it to flow into your bodies. Agree to receive from the gift of the wholeness. I remind you to keep taking deep breaths."

I felt the energy of the room rise with the strong frequency of the life force that is centered on the core of the infinite that was in the palms of their hands.

"The power that you feel in your hands, that's you; that's your life force that is increasing from an encounter with the world. I invite you to relax and contract your ring muscles. Stimulate and awaken your sexual energy. If you feel comfortable, you can also consciously flow sexual energy and the energy of pleasure, and simply allow more of the electricity that is passing through you to flow between you with ease. Remember that you are going to channel that energy to support your lives and the creation of the reality that you seek. Keep breathing and agree to be in your full power."

I observed the women and noticed what was happening: the expression on their faces and the energy that was flowing between them. I saw that Ruth was a little bent over and I sent strengthening energy to her. Immediately I saw her straighten up. I felt the devotion of all to the exercise and the penetrating looks in their eyes that stared into the depths of the soul. I saw Beth's difficulty as she opened and closed her eyes every so often, and I sensed the strong energy flowing in the room and between my hands and Ellie's.

I shivered, took a deep breath, and kept talking. "Great. Now, say your intention. Say it out loud, or in your hearts. Let the energetic wave form and be present. Let those ripples that you feel so strongly in your hands vibrate out clearly into the universe with determination."

I took some more breaths and felt that the women could contain more: "Now, only one of you share in first person with positivity and without negative words, your personal intention. The other woman will hold the intention for her, and together in confidence and determination you will send and reverberate that intention to the universe. You can feel, sense, and imagine the intention create vibrating waves of intention like a ripple."

After a few moments of silence had passed Amber said: "Wow, that is so strong, I'm going to explode any moment."

I asked her to close her eyes and when she was able to contain it to open them once again. "Now, please swap roles. One shares their intention and the other reverberates it out to the universe," I said, and I devoted myself to uttering my intention.

They remained like this for a few moments and then I felt something in me that asked to close the energy. I said: "Take another deep breath; feel what is happening between your hands and breath and take a few moments to feel it. This is a real experience of your powers. I want us to start working with that power more and more, so that you learn to move with the power and derive pleasure from it to create your own reality in your lives. It's a tremendous power. Please thank one another with your eyes and then, slowly, put down your hands."

I looked at them while they showed gratitude to each other with kind and good eyes. The room was quiet and teeming with powerful energy and vitality. Gently, they let go of each other's hands. Some of them hugged and then returned to the circle.

"You are welcome to imagine yourselves sitting with your partner when you flow sexual energy between one and other. Describe what is happening to you. Are you giving and flowing sexual energy, or agreeing and receiving sexual energy?"

Amber responded: "I think that if I would have kept my hands there for one moment longer, I would have flown like a rocket into space."

"That's your power, dearest. You have powers to move things like a rocket full of the energy of life. Here something to practice; hold your tools so that you may truly contain your power." I looked at her lovingly and asked: "Is there anyone else that wants to share what they went through?"

"This is the first time in my life that I have done something like this," Ruth answered my call. "I feel that I have much more to practice to enhance it and allow myself to create reality through it. I felt power in my hands in a way that I have never felt before. I really hope that I will have someone to practice it with," she said in passing.

"Ruth, see how beautiful you are. Do you really think that you won't have anyone to try that with?!" Iris said in response.

"It's not just about being in a couple, but about finding someone that wants to be a partner in every aspect," Ruth said with sadness.

"I am sure you're going to find that," said Iris. "If you were brave enough to get up and go and had the courage to come to a workshop that's called 'Empowered Vulva' you will also have the wisdom to find the right partnership. Aside from that I think that exercise we just did you don't have to do with a boyfriend. I would meet you once a month to practice," said Iris with a sweet smile, adding: "I do a lot with my hands, I feel energy and sometimes I treat people. What I felt today was outstanding and totally different from putting my hands on someone and treating them. That was really an incredible sensation that I want to do again."

Noa looked at me as though she wanted to talk. I smiled at her. "That was moving; I cried from the sheer emotion of it. I don't totally understand what we did and how it's connected to creating a reality. I felt a wave and something very strong happening between our hands that beamed outwards. Sometimes it confuses me. I think that it could be easier for me if we began with the role of the giver for a few minutes, and then the receiver, and at the end to let each other flow together. That would be a little bit more gradual."

I looked at her in gratitude and took a deep breath: "I feel that the experience was beyond words. I would be happy for you to share with me how the exercise reverberated in your daily lives in the future. As with anything, the more you practice, the more it will turn into a tool that can be available for you in your day-to-day lives."

I was surprised that Beth hadn't shared anything until now. Usually, she was the first to respond. She was very quiet. I looked at her and she appeared as though she had been enveloped by a ball of light, tranquil and full to the brim. I moved my gaze to fall on Ellie. She started to speak.

"In the beginning, I had a voice of doubt within me. I didn't really understand what we had to do. I gave you my hands. Entering such an intimate space to face you wasn't easy for me. I felt myself avoiding looking at you. I felt that you were with me completely and present with each of the other women in the circle as well. I was in awe from that skill. It was hard for me to succumb to your gaze that penetrated my soul. Afterwards, something changed. Suddenly, I was one with the current that flowed through me and I totally lost all sense of where my hands began and where they ended; they really merged to become one. All that energy turned into a huge orb of power that was so much more than Ellie or Michal or the two together. We created this mighty essence, so I wonder what will happen to the intention that I placed. I felt strong movement like a ripple that catapulted outside of me. I felt a need to meet the world and have a huge impact on it."

I thanked her for her comment and said: "It was very special and empowering to be with you. The mix of guiding the exercise and holding hands was not easy for me either. To be present with the power between our hands and continue to hold the space was challenging. I too experienced the difficulty of giving in to the look of love when it bears into my eyes for a long time; it fills me with embarrassment and discomfort. I am still learning about my agreement to be in intimacy with the infinite look of love that flows to me. I wish for more of it, so that I may stay in the space of love." I finished my speech, looked at Beth, and said: "Do you want to share anything with us?"

"Yes," she said, quietly, "Truthfully, I didn't feel anything. When Amber told me that she is about to explode, I couldn't understand what she was talking about. I couldn't feel a thing. At the beginning I got stressed and I decided to breathe into my vulva. I focused on relaxing my face and then I simply felt — it's not nice to say — tickling in my vulva. I think that was pleasure. For a moment I got stressed and then I told myself that I agree to contain whatever was going on and suddenly I had this nice feeling in my body. I focused on agreeing to receive pleasure in my body and to give love. There's a chance that I even got wet in my vagina and that is really new. I would be so happy to revive my sex life, and I might even prefer to start calling it love-making as you refer to it."

"Thank you for sharing," I said and smiled at her with a lot of appreciation. "You are the wisdom of the tribe, carrying for us the age of wisdom and understanding. It is so much fun that your life liquids have awoken. I wish you more of this. Perhaps you should practice this exercise with your partner? All the while, agree from the get-go that you stay with clothes on and give each other your hands, placing the intention to channel sexual energy that will flow between you and create more life. Make love in a different way. What do you say?"

Beth laughed out loud and said: "Why not, I hope and I pray that he cooperates with me."

"I think that it will be worth it for him to cooperate with you," I said.

"I have to add something," said Ruth. "I'm a doctor and deal with technology all the time. I feel that there is new tech in what we just learned. I am still not sure how it will influence my life, but it's clear to me that this is something that must reach more people."

I breathed deeply. "I know, and I never have the courage to say that out loud. Thank you."

I looked around me. Everyone looked different: relaxed, enlightened, more comfortable in their own skin.

"Picture a reality that is based on awareness and choice. You experience full power in your life, with your open heart and with the ability to express and communicate your feelings. Picture a reality of connection to your intuition and clear knowledge with living, pulsating, and vibrating sexuality that radiates easily with a sense of home on earth!

"Picture a life in which our full and complete power is available to us; a life where we are aware of the great power of creation and allow it to flow through us in agreement of being a vessel for that power of light and a whole being that vibrates the loving frequency of Creation. How will your life play out? What will happen in the world?"

"We imagine, determined, and feel the world in this existence, and we bring it to life and to the presence. How do our relationships look? Be with this statement watch it take place here and now on the earth."

I gave them some time to imagine, dream, and jump into the potential future. I placed a paper, pen, and colors in their hands, and said: "Draw your ideas and write the visions that you saw." They slowly opened their eyes and started to draw. It felt like a time that is beyond time as we know it. I drew too. I was delighted in that moment for the silence and creativity that had been conceived in the space.

After 20 minutes or so, I said: "Darlings, we have come to the end of the workshop. Let's take a quarter of an hour break and meet back here together with the picture we drew for our closing circle."

The sun's light on a winter afternoon entered the rounded space of the yurt. A sunbeam passed through the crystal, creating lots of colorful, jubilant dots of light around the room. The women got up to use the bathroom, make tea, and go outside for fresh air. I felt the atmosphere of finality in the air. Everyone was a little more self-assured, processing the journey she had gone through as felt by their body language and the conversations between the women. A special and pleasant intimacy had been created during the last two days.

*I recognize that my sexual energy is part of the whole being that I am! I consciously choose for my sexual energy to be available to me to fulfill my unique creation in the world and support the creation of my life's reality. Thank you!*

# CONCLUSION

I placed a candle in the center of the circle in the middle of the sacred space. We all sat down, each person in the space that had become their place over the course of the last two days. I took a deep breath, smiled, and said: "I invite you all, for this last part, to move to a new spot, different from where you sat during the workshop. This will give you a new angle from which to see the space and the other women here with you." They all looked at me with astonishment. Amber got up first and moved to sit next to Noa. One by one, the women got up and built a totally new formation in the circle.

"I am lighting this candle to wrap up the day so that it may light up and warm our hearts," I said. "I hope that it may enlighten us on our paths to becoming the sexuality that we are. Each one of us is a woman learning to stand in her power and learning how to empower, release, and relax their vulvas!"

I smiled and lit the candle, sitting back down and saying: "To finish up, I would like everyone to show their drawings and share how they feel leaving today, as well as what they are taking away with them."

"I would like to start," said Noa. She showed everyone her drawing, a river where a naked woman was swimming happily in the water. "I dream of a world where all women can leisurely bathe naked in a river joyously, where no-one will even think about peeping at them. They are safe, innocent, and truly happy!" She said, with yearning and a smile. "The main gift that I received was the ability to talk more openly about my sexuality and managing to say words that I never dared to say along with things that sat deep within my heart and my vulva. I go home with that intention to talk more and to connect and be in connection with the sexual woman that I am. Thank you to Michal and to all of you."

Amber went after her: "As you can all see, I drew a lake of women coming with jugs to bring water back to the village. It reminds me of sights I saw in India. Mostly I hear their laughter and feel their solidarity and sisterhood! I dream of a world in which all women will belong to a supportive society, where they can support each other and be at peace together. I received many gifts here. The first is the deepening of the breath to my vaginal area and the second: creating less drama from my encounters with men and my dates with them. I learned to talk less about all that with my girlfriends, and instead breathe it all inwards and agree to feel self-love in the knowledge that my love will come soon!"

I added, "I invite you to take responsibility in your day-to-day life; to breathe deep breaths into your vagina and to pay heed to the words that you use to speak to yourself and to the world."

"Your love is waiting for you at the door!" Beth said to her, smiling. "I learnt, that..." she stood and started to let out sighs as she raised her hands, letting them drop downwards in a flap. "I need to release and to let go." Beth sat back down smiling and carried on: "Honestly, you broke so many of my old thought patterns. I want to thank everybody here for supporting me; I leave here as a totally different Beth. I am happier and calmer and I have faith that my liquids will flow back to my vagina. Maybe, just maybe, sexual pleasure will come back into my life, or maybe, more accurately, will enter my life!"

"And your drawing?" I asked.

"I drew the sea, birds, sun, and freedom. I hope that there will be a sense of more sexual freedom in the world, but with a lot more recognition of its deep value and the inspiration it can give to life as well as the support it can give us in our lives. Just as the sea gives us power and inspiration, so too can sexuality. Amen. May I remember that I pray that my grandchildren experience their lives like this; free and powerful. May they always be looked at by men with appreciative, respectful, and loving eyes!"

I felt that I wanted her to go a step further and internalize all the information she had received. I asked her: "Which real action do you take responsibility for and plan to bring into your daily life from what you experienced here?

She took a deep breath and answered: "A lot of things, but I think that starting from tomorrow I'll do the muscle exercise of contracting and releasing the pelvic muscles and letting out sighs throughout the day! I loved that; it was so liberating!" she said with a smile of satisfaction.

"It was really moving to witness the process that you went through here during the workshop," said Amber as she looked at her lovingly with full of appreciation.

"I'd like to continue," said Iris as she turned her picture round to face the circle. "I drew a bonfire with a lot of colors and shades that is burning from one side and whispering to the other, revealing secrets, enlightenment, warmth, life forces, and passion. The gift that I received is the many secrets have been revealed to me. You gave over so much information on sexuality that I had no idea even existed. I have a lot more to practice and learn but I feel the 'yes' within me - the inner uttering that I agree to grow. I am going back home and I ask that you pray for me to be able to talk to my husband about the difficulties that come up for me during sexual encounters with him. I hope that he can hear me without getting offended. I hope that our sex life becomes more pleasurable, a lot more playful, and a lot less serious. And something else — I want to be more daring in my work life; to look people straight in the eye and be really present."

I smiled at her in thanks for what she shared and I turned to look at Ruth.

"First of all, I thank the blessed Lord who brought me to this workshop that empowered me so much, and opened up entire worlds before me. I felt that the movement in my pelvis has opened up, and therefore I drew many spirals in a spinning, infinite movement that has no end and no beginning. I feel that I found more balance and healing when it comes to the separation from my ex-husband. There is more acceptance and a sense of real relief within me. I hope this will continue to stay with me in my life. I go home happy and lighter, feeling more womanly and secure to be in this world with my femininity. Thank you! It really is so meaningful for me!" she said with eyes full of gratitude, adding: "I want to thank each one of you for the sisterhood and the good vibes that were created here between us. It was really special for me, and not at all a given."

"You are so special, Ruth," said Carol. "That special something that you brought here really inspired me to dare, too. You are a doctor; you're religious. From my point of view, it is a statement that you came to this workshop with all that we went through together as sisters. I felt very at home next to you, despite how different we are. This is the picture I drew," she said as she showed us a spectacular drawing of a mother holding a baby next to an older girl, smiling at a man standing in front of them.

"My dream is that the world will be one of smiling, dreaming women supporting their family together with the man who creates and brings great abundance. A world where children who are born don't even have a clue as to what the concept of sexual harassment is. That memory has been erased from collective consciousness of both women and men alike. Mothers teach their daughters the secrets of sexuality, blood, and pleasure. Their sons are educated to be men of love that possess a happy, healthy sexuality, while keeping the peace and brotherhood. From this workshop, I received the ability to put that vision into crystal clear words. Thank you!" she said, as tears of emotion trickled down her cheeks.

"Thank you for that moving and important vision," I said. "A huge part of what allowed me to boldly overcome my fears and share all this knowledge on the subject of sexuality was the effort to change the chain of DNA that we bequeath to our children." I looked at Ellie, the youngest of the group, and asked how she sums it all up.

"That sentence is running through my head: 'even a flood cannot extinguish love," she answered. "Love is a fire, a great fire of life that even water cannot extinguish. That is so powerful. The expression 'love making' that you made sure to use instead of the word sex, sexual encounter, intercourse or even to going to bed, moved something in me; it deepened my understanding of the connection between sexuality and love, explaining that through sexuality we can flow so much love through the body. I understood that love making is the material fulfillment of the energy of love. It really moves me to know that sexuality is the key to great pleasure. That's why I drew a flower that looks like a vulva, full of beauty, passion, sexiness, and the stunning simplicity of life! I received the permission to be happy to be who I am, to explore and to experience the sexual being that I am, and even to tell myself that I am sexual and feel really — and I mean really — good about that! I wrote down a vision of a world that is safe for women and men, where my daughters and my grandchildren  know a time where it was not safe to walk alone in the streets. They won't know about fear from rape. A world where sexuality is both healthy and beneficial for both men and women."

"What action do you want to take back and practice in your daily life?" I asked.

She looked at me with a cheeky grin: "I want to practice flowing sexual energy by myself as I pleasure myself while putting in intention. I'm curious about what will happen."

I looked at Ellie and said: "Wonderful!" I exchanged looks with everyone in the room.

With a smile on my face and a lot of emotion and gratitude that fulfills me I said: "I am ending the workshop with a happy heart. These are moments of grace where we cross fears and apprehensions and walk with confidence towards the whole woman that you are. Sexuality is rooted as an important part of our essence, and this part is of great privilege to me."

I took a deep breath, stretched my hands to my sides, and carried on: "Let's join hands. Our right hand faces down in giving, and our left faces upwards in receiving. We'll create a circle of giving and receiving that flows through our whole being, from us to the other and back to us."

Everyone held hands by their sides and created a shared circle.

"Let's breathe in unison, with gratitude in our hearts and an agreement to receive thanks. Notice the frequency and the special vibration that flows between us. We created magic over the last two days together. Give this gift the potential to blend deep into your being. Feel, sense, imagine or think that you are leaving here beating to a new movement in the world, with life forces that support the whole being that you are and specifically, the sexuality that you are. Take a deep breath, and gently let go of your hands and place them on our hearts. Everyone is welcome to bless themselves, silently, between you and the creator. I bless myself and each one of you here with self-love, pleasure, and a deepening in the ability to empower and relax the vulva through breath, through choosing self-appreciation in pleasure and in choosing life."

Everyone kept their eyes closed and placed their hands on their hearts. I let them have a few moments of internal pledges. I felt the deep prayer in my body that everyone carried in their hearts and I spoke again: "Let's have a group hug, place our hands behind the backs of the person next to us across from their hearts, and say together out loud with confidence, happiness, and love: I choose life. I am a sexual woman; I am happy in my sexuality, and I am alive!"

We stood close to one another and a powerful wave of energy flowed between us. I felt the statement that we made together create expanding ripples that spread out to the whole world, the generations of women that once were, and the women of the future.

"That's it. We've wrapped up, beloveds. Thank you!" I exclaimed. I looked at everyone in their eyes while smiling and had so much love in my heart. We gently let go of our hands and hugged each other. One by one, the women went their separate ways. I was left at home alone, with a feeling of fullness and deep gratitude for the privilege of accompanying women on their journey towards themselves. I had a prayer in my heart for future generations, for the boys and girls that will be born into a world of joy, simplicity, and comfort around the most powerful energy we have in our life: sexual energy, pure, radiant, and sparkling, wrapped in love and full of life!

*I choose that, the people closest to me and the people of the world all raise their vibration and live in recognition that sexual energy is part of the powerful wholeness and holiness that we are. We express our personal sexual beings with love, wisdom, and respect for ourselves and t those around us.*
*Let there be light!*

# BECOMING VULVACIOUS — SUGGESTIONS AND EXERCISES

There are many ways and possibilities of how to become vulvacious — in other words, to empower, release and relax the vulva. You will find here a list of some of them. Take whatever suits you at this moment in time. Dare to try and experiment. What works for you today may no longer suit you tomorrow, and vice versa. You are invited to leave your comfort zone. When we do things differently from the usual, the change brings something new into our lives.

I ask that you be in clear communication and attentiveness to yourself. There are still many places in the world where women are in real danger if seen in public with their powers. That being said, the world is changing. **Use your wisdom to choose when** it is right for you to be seen in public in your full strength and when it is right to illuminate your light from the inside. It's within you and between you and yourself; you are always free to choose life. It's in your hands!

In order to empower the vulva, it's important to choose to have a relaxed vagina, released from tension, contractions, painful memories that will stimulate you from inside.

Good luck!

**I choose, I learn, and I practice life in awareness of a relaxed, released, liberated, and empowered vulva.**

## PAYING ATTENTION TO THE VULVA

Live a life in awareness and mindfulness of the vulva. Pay attention to your vulva; love her so that there is a connection between your loving heart and your vulva. Kind eyes and good thoughts towards your vulva will lead to deep listening and health.

**I choose, I live in awareness and mindfulness to my vulva!**

## BREATH

Through breath, life flows. Within the word breath in Hebrew sits the word 'soul.' The breath is a tool that enables our soul to be realized in the material, in the body, and in our daily life. We want to bring the soul in through breath and into our vulva. Breathing, awareness of the breath, and conscious breathing is the key to relaxation of the body and the mind.

Why should you consciously breathe into your vulva?

**It connects you to your vulva.**

**It helps to focus your attention on your vulva.**

**It develops the skill to consciously interact and have a dialogue with your vulva.**

**It helps us to remain present and maintain calming thoughts during lovemaking.**

**It increases pleasure during lovemaking.**

**It creates ease, relaxation, and calm.**

**It teaches you to listen to the desires of your vulva.**

**It flows life energy prana-chi to your vulva.**

**It deepens clear communication with your vulva.**

**It releases pain and tension from your vagina.**

**It helps to contain the energy of love.**

# BREATHING THROUGH THE NOSE

Inhale through the nose to the opening of the vagina; the vagina will expand and open.

Exhale out the nose; contract the circular muscles of the vaginal opening, and the vagina will tighten up.

Try resting your hand on your vaginal area for the duration of the exercise.

# INHALATION THROUGH THE MOUTH

Take in air as though you are breathing through a straw to contract the circular muscles upwards. You can ball your palms into a fist as you do this, in a movement that gathers energy from the ground to the hands inwardly.

Exhalation: release the air from the mouth so that the vagina can relax.

# INHALATION AND EXHALATION, GIVING AND RECEIVING

This exercise truly opens the heart and brings the heart and body closer. I recommend doing it with people close to you whom you trust.

Sit opposite one another and hold hands. The right hand holds the right hand of your partner and the left hand holds their left hand. The four palms are placed on each other, so that the form of eight is created, with the palms in the center.

Close your eyes.

Do the following, ten times:

Focus on the left hand, inhale, and state: "I agree to receive. I agree to be entered and connected."

Focus on the right hand, exhale, and state: "I agree to give. I agree to enter and to connect."

The flow of energy and air passes with awareness to the heart. The heart is part of the flow of the eight form. If you feel comfortable, and it is appropriate, you are welcome to consciously flow your sexual energy through the infinite that flows between you. Open your eyes and look deep into the soul of the person facing you.

# PRACTICING PRESENCE

Life in presence in the here and now is a peaceful and calmer life. Even when there is drama, being present in the body enables us to develop the ability to act out of a place of inner peace and clarity. There are many methods available to teach presence. Adopt the one that makes you happy and practice it. Being present during love making is pleasant but sometimes challenging as we encounter with inner truths that aren't always nice for us to experience or witness. Choosing presence in the moment and agreeing to deal with whatever comes up inside of us gives us an opportunity to release contractions in the vagina and allows for more relaxation and communication to be present in our life. The healing comes and along with it comes more energy for health.

Deep breaths, releasing sighs, and the connection with our center deepen our ability to be in the present moment.

**I choose to live life fully present in my body — I am here!**

## SIGHS

Releasing sighs is one of the more significant tools to allow the vagina to relax, release overthinking and tension, and especially enable being present. Sighs come out spontaneously and unconsciously during love making and allow for us to stay present in the moment of the here and now.

Take a deep breath; you can also raise your hands upwards, and release your hands as you let out a sighing sound. Do this a few times over.

## MEDITATION FOR BALANCING, STRENGTHENING, AND RELAXING THE VULVA

You are invited to activate the barcode to listen to the meditation:

# RELAXED JAW — RELAXED VAGINA

The jaw muscles are both the strongest muscles and the most frequently engaged. When you relax your jaw, the body naturally starts to relax and release, and the vagina follows. Take the tongue from the upper palate and allow the lower jaw to sink down. Agree to relax and release the accumulated tension in the face and jaw area. The circular muscles in the mouth are connected to the circular vagina muscles and they influence each other. Therefore, when the jaw is relaxed, the vagina is relaxed.

**I choose to live in awareness that my jaws are relaxed.**

# DEDICATION

When you give in to softness, the vagina softens, and a man of love can enter into you and you can devote yourself to love, pleasure, and to the light and knowledge that he is pouring into you. Together you can melt into the infinite, growing together and allowing more wisdom and universal love to come through you both.

These are the moments of grace. They can come to you when you agree to relax, release the contractions, and surrender.

**I choose to dedicate myself to soft, loving, and pleasurable sexuality. Thank you, thank you, thank you!**

# WILD WOMAN

You are sexual, instinctive, and alive.[17] Give space for the passion for life to flow through your veins; put the shame away and find space for the animal inside you in a supportive environment that can contain and hold you where you feel relaxed and safe. Wildness can be expressed by touching yourself gently, moaning, shouting, laughing, crying, purring, sighing, making love on the ground, and more...

Every woman has her own shade of wildness. Let the wildness that is inside of you be expressed naturally, with your exact magic that makes you who you are. A vulva can be empowered and relaxed when you honor all your parts, even the wild ones.

**I choose to give space in my life to the wild woman that I am.**

# DANCING WITH HIPS

Our joints are made for movement. They are the junctions through which a lot of energy passes through and, naturally, the junctions hold a lot of tension. When we don't move them enough, they get stuck. When we are anxious, ashamed, or suppress our sexual energy, our hips and pelvic joints contract and sometimes even lock. Therefore, it's recommended to increase mobility there by turning your hips left to right and backwards and forwards, in full rotations, so that the life energy in the pelvis is set in motion. This practice is blessed both for use in daily life and during love making. Belly dancing is an exceptional, magnificent, and recommended

17. In Hebrew, the word 'alive,' 'haya,' also means animal or beast, leaving room to maneuver between the language of life and the language of the animal.

way to offload burdens and tensions from the pelvic area and more specifically from the vagina and womb. I suggest putting on some music, dancing at home with yourselves or with a dance group, learning more about freeing the pelvis through movement!

## CONTRACTION AND RELEASING

The circular muscles in the vagina and anus are located in the center of the body. The conscious practice of contracting and releasing allows you to hold the physical experience of your center, strengthen the pelvic floor muscles. and provide vitality and strength. When you tighten and release the vaginal muscles on a regular basis, your sexual energy will be available for you as a powerful tool to support you. You can experience pleasure without directly engaging in intercourse. As such, if you are in the midst love making and consciously clench up and release the vagina, you increase not only your own sexual pleasure, but your partner's, too.

## PLACING A HAND ON THE VAGINAL AREA

Place a hand on your vaginal area, allowing the heat of the palm of your hand to flow to her. It makes her happy and relaxes her — and you.

# MENSTRUATION

### Track, rest, and be grateful for the gift

Tracking your cycle and knowing when your blood is due, along with your personal familiarity with your distinctive nature and with your lunar time, helps you to know when your menses comes and to plan your time accordingly. It is important to understand that there is a period in the month for rest and another time intended for action. When you learn to allow for the rest deep within yourself in quiet full knowledge, it takes away any tension from the womb and pelvic area and lets the vagina bleed her sacred blood in peace.

During your menses time, take time out to rest.

Your blood time is not supposed to hurt, but it does requires rest for your body and soul. I invite you to derive pleasure from this time. With the blood that comes you can cleanse and convey your intent to release from your life any issues worrying you, letting these worries end. Menstruation is a time of respite from the intensity of everyday life; a time or being in the company of other woman, converging inwards, and taking it down a gear. This is a time for daydreaming.

### For those who choose more depth and connection with the blood

Collect the blood and water the garden, especially plants in the garden that need strengthening. When the conditions allow, you can bleed straight into the earth, collect the blood, and use it for a ritual around the fire and on the ground. Bless the ground around your home and water the earth with your blood.

For the courageous ones — drink it (you can mix the blood with a fruit shake). Touch your blood with joy, draw with the blood, and let its texture bring you joy. It has so much healing and power. It revives us and gives us strength.

A woman who honors and respects her blood allows her power to be present in her body! Hatred of the blood constricts the vagina. The love for blood empowers the power of that area in your body, which is the seat of your life force.

**I choose to love my menstruation blood. I awaken my DNA to life, respect, and appreciation for the power of the blood that passes through me. I live in my full power!**

## THE SONG OF THE VAGINA

Singing, sounds, and intuitive voices are tools that enable liberation, relaxation, letting go, releasing of tension, expansion, opening of the heart, and allowing a feeling of spiritual elation! The circular muscles in the mouth are connected to the circular muscles in the pelvis. When we sing the mouth moves with a fluidity and you devote yourself to song; your vagina sings too and it relaxes and collects the circular muscles in the body.

When you sing and your mind lets go of thoughts — your vagina relaxes. When we sing low tones, the vagina and the pelvic floor become an echo chamber; the area relaxes and rests, enabling oneself to devote oneself to the vitality and life that flows and moves through the vagina.

For a woman during childbirth, for example, it is recommended to sing low tones and connect to the lower parts of the body and the earth. Her mind will calm down and relax and the vagina can expand and open up in preparation for childbirth. The same thing happens during love making; when there's too much going on and there is internal stress on an emotional or physical level, you can always sing. The vagina will let go, and the opening will expand and allow the penis to penetrate pleasantly into the yoni's sacred space.

# SINGING TO THE VULVA

Another great tip to relax the vulva: the man can place his mouth on the vaginal lips or on the Venus mound (the bone above the vulva) and sing a pleasing song to the vulva. The vulva and the entire pelvic area turn into an echo chamber and the vulva can rest and relax, relishing in the pleasantness of the sound that vibrates her vulva.

I give permission before entry into my vagina

Create a relationship in which the man, during a sexual encounter, asks permission to enter and connect with you. The request can be done through the use of clear words, an inquiring touch, or a look asking for your permission. Your answer can also be given clearly in words, touch, or a look. The yes is complete when the vagina, the heart, and the mind all say yes to making love. Through the request and your subsequent agreement, the vagina will relax.

**I listen to myself and my body, trust myself, and know how to say yes when I want full sexual contact. I also learn to say no when sexual contact does not suit me.**

# SMILE

A smiling mouth is a smiling vagina! The mouth and the vagina are directly linked through the lips and circular muscles that are situated in the pelvis and the face. Smiling is healthy in every respect. Smile throughout your life; to yourself and during love making. During childbirth it is very noticeable, physically. The moment that a woman manages even a hint of a smile, the contractions immediately become much less painful and the opening of the cervix happens more easily. Smile as much as possible throughout your life! This makes it easier and happier in the heart and in the vagina!

# THE POWER OF IMAGINATION

With the help of imagination, you can support the relaxing and release of excess energy and contractions in the vagina.

Before the practice, breathe deep breaths for a few minutes while sitting or lying down.

Only after you have entered a feeling of inner peace, begin this exercise of guided imagination.

Here are some options to practice:

- Imagine water that washes, cleanses, and purifies the anxieties and contractions from the vagina.
- Imagine a heart sitting in your vulva that illuminates your vagina with loving light.
- Imagine sunlight shining through your vagina.
- Imagine a pattern in the infinity shape flowing between your heart and your vulva, flowing love to the vulva while the vulva flows essential life energy and passion to the heart.
- Imagine your vulva is happy and full of colorful flowers that adorn it and turn it into a gate of life, joy, and celebration.
- Imagine sweet fairies coming to your vagina with glittering gold fairy dust that cleanses and purifies excess energy.

You are invited to let your imagination run wild and take your vulva on a journey of healing.

You can do these imagination exercise alone by yourself or as preparation for love making.

# SELF-PLEASURE

When you pleasure yourself, your vulva enjoys it and you enjoy it! Touch yourself with love, passion, attention, gentleness, and intention of having intimate and loving time with yourself. The word masturbation has a lot of negative connotations; guilt, fear, and hiding. Therefore, I choose to use the words self-pleasure. Allot a calm and quiet time to pleasure yourself; a time where you can make love with yourself that is not dependent on somebody else; only you and the Creator.

When you investigate loving sexual encounters with and by yourself, you are making room to meet with your partner during love making from a place of not needing another person in order to enjoy yourself. It frees dependencies and brings a release from the expectation that pleasure will come from outside.

Self-pleasure deepens your personal and intimate connection with yourself and enables a more relaxed, freeing, and pleasurable sexual encounter with another.

One of the more important tips in breaking patterns of guilt while self-pleasuring is to touch yourself in a different position, so that you can free yourself from automatic movements and thinking patterns. In this way, pleasure has more room in which to enter.

**I choose to live in pleasure with myself.**
**I pleasure myself and**
**I love myself!**

# UNDERWEAR

Underwear is designed to cover our vulva, protect it, warm it, and prevent any mingling with energies that are undesirable. They provide a clear boundary, make it possible to put on a pad to collect the blood inside us, and prevent the discharge from our vaginas to chaff between our legs. Discharge varies in amount depending on our time of the month in our cycle.

Apart from the times where we really need underwear, it is better to be without them. They dressed us in underwear to defend us but also to hide us, prevent the continuous and gushing flow of life energy from running through our bodies, and to shut off and block our vaginal opening from entry and exit of the energetic life flow. I strongly recommend you free yourself from underwear for the majority of the year and use them thoughtfully when you really need them.

At first, start by sleeping at night without underwear.

In any case, when you choose to wear underwear, cozy, comfortable cotton underwear is best. It should not be tight on the body.

# SIT LESS WITH YOUR LEGS CROSSED

Practice and get used to placing two feet on the ground and allowing the energy of life to flow through you in a free flow. If you want to close your legs, check with yourself as to why... Is it from force of habit? Or perhaps you are having an unbearable experience and you feel sexual energy is hard to contain.

When you feel under threat act with resolve, will, and confidence to remove the threat. When you feel sexual energy — take a deep breath. You are glad that the energy of life is flowing through you and you thank it for reminding you of your choice in life.

**I choose and I declare to the world that I agree to feel and sense through my vulva. I listen to my vulva. I communicate the sincere and authentic will of my vulva!**

## RECLAIMING THE RIGHT TO LIFE IN POWER

Host a ritual with yourself; a ceremony of the restoration of your rights to live in power as a woman on this earth. You are welcome to take some quiet time to yourself, and to call for support from the creator during your ceremony. You can light a candle. You are welcome to take an object that represents your insecurities and bury it in the ground. Declare to the universe, out loud, that you choose life in your full power.

**I choose and I walk confidently in the world. I resolutely learn about life from a place of appreciation, confidence, and self-respect.
I live in my full power!**

## CLEAR BOUNDARIES

A vulva can be relaxed when she knows that her signals are listened, when she says "no" in an unequivocal way, and when there is disrespectful entry or penetration into her space. This includes disrespectful words, a disrespectful look, and a disrespectful penetration by the penis into the vagina. If you didn't say "no" and froze up, please forgive yourself with compassion, and help yourself to receive help to release the constriction that resulted.

# SUNLIGHT

Sunlight has the tremendous ability to charge your body with *prana* — life energy. Most of the time, the vaginal area is in the dark and sunlight rarely touches her. Once in a while it is recommended to find a quiet place where you can feel at ease and safe to open your legs to the light of the sun and let the warm and pleasant sunshine directly onto your vagina to recharge her with life energy.

# PURIFYING WITH SAGE

Sage is a plant with purifying qualities that can clear negative energies. When you go through a situation that causes contractions, find yourself in a space where you have not been respected, or feel negative energy around you, it is good to light dried sage leaves and let the smoke purify around your body and vulva.

# DIPPING WHILE NAKED IN THE SEA OR A SPRING

There are no words to describe the blessing of a naked dip in nature in a spring or in the sea. The dip brings blessings to the body and specifically to the vagina. When water touches the vaginal opening directly, the water supports a woman's increased ability to live with a relaxed vagina. The more you immerse yourself in a body of water that is closer to the water source, the higher and more purifying the water frequency will be. The body of water welcomes you inside. Entering the water starts usually with your feet and it moves upwards. The water meets the center of the body starting from the feet, the pelvis, and the vagina that expands in the face of such an encounter with water. This is likened to a womb within a womb, and it is so feminine and enveloping. In a shower, water comes down on you from above and touches a different place each time. The water invades you and doesn't allow for much expansion. A natural pool of water caresses you from every direction and enables relaxation.

# YONI MASSAGE — MASSAGING THE VULVA

This is a sacred ritual for vaginal healing, pleasure, recuperation from pain, and anxieties that the vulva carries within her. Yoni massage is a wonderful way to lead a woman to healing and relaxation of the vulva. This practice is around the vaginal area, the pelvis, the hip joints, and within the vaginal tunnel. The massage greatly supports the ability to relax the vagina and let go of contractions that sit inside her. The massage releases deep emotions that are encoded inside the vagina, emotions from this life and collective emotions of women that passed from mother to daughter.

I mostly recommend that you learn how to give a yoni massage to yourself. There are workshops where you can learn how to do a yoni massage on yourself or with your partner, so you can incorporate the yoni massage as preparation for love making. You can also receive a yoni massage from a therapist, of which there are a growing number who know the art of sacred massage for our sacred genitals.

Please note! During the yoni massage always listen to your body and to your inner limits. A yoni massage does not include penetration of the penis into the vagina or oral sex. A yoni massage can only include full sexual contact if it is with your partner.

# PRESSING ON THE VENUS MOUND

The Venus mound is the area that sits above the labia's lips, the pubic bone, where our pubic hair grows. You can massage yourself by pressing on the Venus mound, the area of the groin and the outer and inner labia's lips. You can press with your fingers on that area caringly and sensitively. If the pressure hurts, try to pause there and breathe into the pain. I discovered that it's a process that relieves the stress and pain and impacts the rest of our body and on our moods. You are welcome to try!

# ENERGY TRANSFORMATION

This is an internal choice about taking responsibility for the process of energetic cleaning of the vulva. Letting go and cleansing brings about a transformation of fear in faith, pain in pleasure, and light in loads. It can happen when you agree to be in acceptance, in gratitude, in an embrace, in love, and in presence with the fear, the pain, and the difficulties. From there comes transformation.

**The way to perform transformation:**
1. Breathe into the vagina, identify the pain, and breathe into the painful place.
2. Hug, love, respect, and include the pain that arises.
3. Be grateful for the pain.
4. Exercise self-love and acceptance — exactly and precisely for when you are afraid/in pain/in difficulty.
5. Have a conversation with the pain/fear/overload. What support does it need right now?
6. Listen to the vagina, stay with her, breathe into the pain, and release.

7. Nourish the pain/fear/overload with whatever it asks from you.
8. Have a conversation with the pain. What does the pain want to tell you? What can you learn from it?
9. Nourish the vagina with love.
10. Allow space within you for transformation (it won't always come; be patient with yourself on your journey!)

Another way to transform is to ask for help from the universe alongside a deeper prayer to release and purify out of respect for the existence and presence in your life!

## LOVE EGG

This is a stone in an egg-shaped stone that is connected to a string. You insert it into your vaginal canal. The act of holding the love egg in your vagina strengthens your pelvic floor muscles, increases sensitivity, control, and relaxation of your vagina. It enhances your sex life and your ability to orgasm, and gives vitality to your womb after the period of menstruation. I recommend learning from a teacher how to use the egg in the most supportive way.

## CONVERSATIONS WITH THE VULVA

You can talk to any organ in the body, and ask after its wellbeing and what it wants to tell you. Many of us aren't used to conducting an internal dialogue with our body parts. We would be surprised and delighted if we open dialogue with our bodies and learn how it answers us, honestly, with answers that may surprise us or, be obvious. Talk to your vagina; ask her how she is and what she wants to tell you this morning or evening. Ask her if she enjoys love making, or if penetration suits her in this moment.

If you have a vaginal infection, ask your vagina what she wants to tell you. This way, it will become easier and easier to recognize when your vagina is freezing up. It will also be easier to recognize what she wants, when she is open to love making, when the pace is too fast for her, and when touch doesn't feel quite right.

The vagina has a lot of wisdom. Her answer can come in the form of clear words, in pictures that arise in the mind's eye, in a blatant feeling without words, and in clear sensations inside the vagina. You are welcome to learn the language of your vagina!

**I choose life in clear communication with my vagina and connect with my sincere and authentic desires — both mine and hers!**

# SERENITY

Relax into the sensations that you feel in your vulva. Live with respect and appreciation for the life flow that passes through you to bring sexual arousal, pleasure, or numbness.

When a wave of sexuality comes, tell yourself that it is nice, and that you choose a life in pleasure. Breathe into the feeling and release. Calm your thoughts and breathe. Declare: "I live in serenity and ease with the sexual being that I am."

## VULVA IN THE MIRROR

Look at your vulva in a mirror and befriend her. When you observe her, identify your feelings. Practice curiosity and admiration for the appearance of your vulva. If a feeling of rejection arises, smile to yourself and accept your authentic feelings. Tell your vulva that you love her, and that she is beautiful!

## FERTILITY AWARENESS METHOD

There are courses where you can learn to connect to the process of conscious fertility. You learn to recognize the cyclical rhythm of your body and its exact signals as to when you are fertile and when you are not. When you learn your cycle and listen to it, you know when your fertile days are and when there is no chance that you will get pregnant. You take responsibility to connect to your inner rhythm. Your knowledge and experience sooths, relaxes, releases, and empowers your vulva.

**I choose and I learn my unique cycle. Thank you!**

# BALANCING THE MASCULINE AND FEMININE WITHIN

It is easier to relax into your vulva power when there is internal balance between the masculine and the feminine inside you. There will be less tension and inner struggle and more of a life of cooperation.

**Ways to balance the masculine and feminine:**
- Inner willingness to go through an inner process of life in balance between these two wonderful forces.
- Participate or create a forgiveness ritual for yourself between the masculine and feminine.
- Feel, think, and imagine that the infinity symbol ∞ flows between the right and left side of your body. The symbol has the intention to balance the male and female energies within you.
- Declare the intentions for balance and partnership between the male and female...

*With the full support of the universe, I
choose to live in balance and cooperation
between the masculine and feminine energy
within me. Thank you!*

●

*I live in a world where the masculine power
lives in peace with the feminine power.
The masculine energy trusts the feminine
energy,
and the feminine energy trusts the
masculine energy.
There is recognition of the importance of
each one of these forces.
These forces exist together in peace,
harmony, cooperation, and mutual respect
for one another.*

●

*I choose, the powerful woman that I am,
to live happily with a powerful man — a
man of love.*

# BLOOD RELEASE | NAAMA TEVA KAUFMAN

We have the ability to excrete bodily fluids as we wish and to control them. Urine and feces should not simply escape. When the body signals that we need to empty ourselves, we recognize the sensation and immediately go to the toilet. This is how it's supposed to be with our menstrual blood. Over the last thousand years, natural signs and sensations have faded from memory. Ways of absorption have been invented that actually cut off the sensations of blood flow. Learning and re-remembering the sensations of the coming blood release enables a woman to recognize the signs and signals and release the blood when it comes.

During your menstrual days, you can learn and increase awareness of your blood flow. When the blood waves ask to be emptied, go to the bathroom or go outside to empty your blood on the earth.

Awareness to the blood waves and the responsibility you take for emptying the blood deepens your connection with your body and helps you to live with a vulva that feels like she is being listened to and is sensitive to the movement of fluids inside her.

**I choose, I live attentively to the movement of fluids in my body.**

## INTENTION BEFORE MAKING LOVE

Before lovemaking or during, have an intention, and state it in your heart or out loud. It is an intention that can be specifically related to lovemaking or to anything that you want to magnetize in your lives.

**I choose and I manage my personal energy, which contains within it my sexual energy. I ride the wave of my sexual energy and create reality in my life!**

## TRANSFORMING VICTIM-LIKE VULVA TO SELF-LOVE

Oftentimes, the victim-like vulva recreates the same story in her life over and over again.

1. Transmit endless love to your vulva.
2. Practice and strengthen your skills of listening to your vulva.
3. Talk to her courageously and with inner confidence.
4. Stop criticizing the poor, unfortunate, and suffering vulva and instead start to truly love the victim that she is. Recite an infinite amount of times: I am loved and I am a truly beloved victim. Thank her and her victimhood.
5. Don't abandon the victim that comes up inside you. Every time that you fail to relate to her pain and suffering with respect, she experiences abandonment. Say hello to her, hug her, and talk to her with words of love.
6. Say thanks from the bottom of your heart for her victimhood. She mostly comes to keep you from getting hurt, even if at a certain point this is no longer serving. The original intention was rooted in protecting you.

7. Agree and take inner responsibility to overcome the fear and choose life. Peel endlessly the layers of fear and victimhood that sit inside our beings. With tolerance, a lot of love, compassion, and acceptance free the patterns of victimization that trigger us both consciously and unconsciously.

This liberation is expressed in our daily lives: in our sexual lives, our love lives, our encounters with men, our encounters with ourselves and with our partners, encounters with parents, encounters with children, and encounters with G-d.

You are invited to agree to grow within the most intimate and close relationships in your life and to create the experience of closeness, peace, harmony, and unity. We live in a time where the frequency of victimhood and feeling unfortunate is found very deep within the society in which we live. Therefore, the transformation of the victimized energy into one of life coming from a place of self-love asks us to be very determined, focused, preserving, patient, self-loving, willing to change. Choosing life for a vital, pulsating, and breathing vulva is a choice for a vulva that loves herself exactly as she is. This is a choice for when she is in her power and loved and also when she is feeling unfortunate and like a victim.

**With all that I am, I choose, activate, and stimulate my cellular DNA in all worlds, times, dimensions, and levels for a life with self-love!**

# ESSENTIAL OILS THAT BOOST FEMALE ENERGY

There are essential oils which, combined with a base oil, have a smell or application on the pelvic region that has a calming effect and awakens desire and vitality. Rose oil, jasmine, and neroli ylang are great oils that open the heart and stimulate the senses.

Cinnamon oil strengthens the uterine region. Lavender and Chamomile oil soothes and relieves pain and tension.

It is recommended to consult with an aromatherapist to find the right oil.

# SISTERHOOD OF WOMEN

Creating a supportive women's circle in your life is an essential factor that enables you to relax your vulva during menstruation. It is also essential for when you want a friend that listens to the secrets of your heart, and to share the challenging and joyful moments in life.

You are welcome to organize a regular monthly session, at the birth of the new moon or during the full moon, each time with a different subject under discussion. Perhaps there is one person that can lead the circle, or each time someone different can guide the circle around a certain subject. It can be a sharing circle or a ceremony which you hold together. It is worthwhile to create a permanent meeting place. I recommend a regular circle that includes between four to twelve women. Of course, the circle can be bigger, but then the leadership needs to be very, very focused because the circle can become too long and tedious.

# STEAM BATHS FOR THE PELVIS | KEREN LEVANA

This is an amazing ancient technique used to soften the vagina and gently open the pelvis. The technique is meant for cleansing and purification, to invite pleasure, health, connection and love. By using healing herbs and water vapor, we can warm the pelvis. The heat circulates the blood, which begins to soften and open. The steam cleanses the tissues and internal organs, and the healing aroma of the plants purifies and soothes each plant with the medicine it brings.

This practice is simple and each one of us can apply it in our own home.

In choosing the plants:

Recommended plants include rosemary, lavender, thyme, basil, oregano, rose, chamomile plants, and calendula. If you choose plants that are off this list, **please make sure that they definitely do not have toxicity in them.** Come to the plants with humility. Smell them, feel the herbs, and check which one of them feels right to you that day at a chosen quantity.

When you pick and cook the plants — ask them for healing that you want for your vulva, womb, vagina, labia lips, and your femininity. This brings in an intention to the process. Start with cooking. Cook a generous handful of fresh or dried herbs in a saucepan with a lid until it boils. Let it sit for another five to ten minutes on a low flame. Wait until the steam is at a pleasant temperature for the pelvis as you sit over the pot at a safe distance with caution. Find a comfortable position or arrange a place to sit where fumes can pass through. Cover yourself with a blanket. This is how you create a kind of sauna for your pelvis. Sit comfortably for at least ten minutes over the steam. When you have finished, get into bed to rest another half-hour or slip into a sweet slumber.

If you want to deepen the practice, every Arvigo therapist — a method of abdominal and lower back massage that helps bring the uterus back to its natural state — can guide and support you. This process is not meant to replace medical treatment.

## BIRTH CLOSURE RITUAL | DASI ELAD

Part of empowering and relaxing your vulva is self-care after childbirth. The pregnancy itself and the end of the childbirth are a process of expansion of the body — the muscles, ligaments, skin, and the tissues, the increased volume of blood, and the softening and opening of the pelvic joints. There is also the process of emotional expansion for the benefit of the new soul that is about to arrive, as well as a spiritual opening to allow the forces of creation to reach and fulfill the miracle of birth. It is a process that changes the entire surface of the pelvic region, including the uterus, the vaginal canal, and the vagina, and sometimes leaves a trauma in the area. Sometimes the pelvic bones and ligaments do not go back to their original shape after the birth, which is a condition that can cause pelvic pain and discomfort. The emotional plane of a woman stays gaping and open which can result in energy loss, confusion, and fatigue. A closing ceremony supports pelvic reorganization and releases tensions in the pelvic area that were created because of the pregnancy and childbirth. The origin of the ritual is from the Mayan culture. The ritual itself symbolizes the end of the pregnancy and the birth on all levels, as well as the closure of the body and the soul, the contracting and returning inside to the center, and the quiet.

As part of the ceremony, the woman gets into a hot bath with medicinal herbs and immediately after that undergoes a deep massage. At the end of the session, she is wrapped in a shroud from head to toe while singing prayers and blessings. The wrapping lasts some 20 minutes to half an hour. In various Native American cultures, it is customary to hold the ceremony at different stages:

there is a custom to do it at the end of the birth itself and there are also those who wait until the bleeding is over. There are places where they do it several times throughout the period of postpartum. It can be done even years after the birth. It is also important to do it after stillbirths and miscarriages.

## CREATION

Crafts, painting, drawing, embroidery, singing, playing music, dancing, writing and any creative activity is a time that nourishes the soul and makes the vulva happy. The vulva is one of the main gateways for the body to express our creativity/creation.

## EARTH

Lie on it, walk barefoot, lie on your back and put stones on you that will help you sink down more towards the earth and let go, receiving the earth's healing medicine.

# DISCOURSE OVER SEXUALITY

Practice your ability to talk about sexuality and about aspects of your sexuality. Converse and talk about your pleasure from sexuality and about the challenges that you have. Get used to talking about sexuality simply, with ease and without shame.

You should talk about it only with people with whom you feel comfortable and safe, like a good girl friend, a close friend, or a partner.

# ACTIVATING INTENTIONS

You are invited to write down your intentions related to your sexuality, femininity, and vulva, and to recite them out loud or by heart with determination and confidence. This way you are strengthening the support of the universe in creating a balanced and joyous vulva!

# CLOSING WORDS

This book began writing itself. I was afraid of writing this text. I feared this book would see the light of day, and knowing that sexuality is part of my being.

For five years this book was woven and embroidered, starting in the second person, moving to the third person and, eventually, evolving to be written in the first person—in a profound covenant with myself to be seen in the world as I am!

To be seen in my challenges, and in my beauty, stubbornness, and tenderness!

To be seen in my sexuality and in my disconnections from it!

To be seen in my divinity and humanity!

I brought this book to light out of my life's mission, so that it may be dedicated to raising my level of awareness and that of humanity's. I have deep knowledge that has been set free. Human beings carry around sexual energy that can bring so much light and peace to the world. This liberation allows our children and grandchildren to live in a better world. The change starts from inside, from the fact that I choose to make this change. This decision affects those around me and influences the entire world!

When I empower and free my vulva, I agree to more feminine essence to dwell within me and give it a place and a presence in my life. I agree to be a tool and container of love. In this choice, I awaken the deep essence of the man, enabling him to give the woman the gift of giving, loving and wholeness. I allow more pleasure to be part of my life! I have had a long journey and I am still going through more and I will pass through even more, in order to fulfil myself to be who I am in this world. Creating this book is part of my agreement to be who I am. I invite you to come and join in the circles, in online courses and ceremonies that I hold.

To deepen your connection to your vulva power throughtr my online courses please scan.

**Cheers, to the empowered and relaxed vulva!**

# ACKNOWLEDGEMENTS & THANKS

I would like to thank the wondrous creation whose hidden ways led me to devote myself to writing this book. Thank you to Iris Yotvat for waking up the women of the Hebrew tribe and instilling the concept of "Leharpot Et Hapot."[18]

Thank you to my mother and my father; from a young age, I was able to talk to them openly about sexuality. Thank you for your endless support in my life. You are always there for me! A huge thanks to my beloved Nitai, my partner for the journey in this life. Thank you for the love, endless support, and shared discoveries. Thank you for facing the challenges that authoring this book brought into our relationship and for the growth of each one of us, as well as our partnership. Thank you to each one of my children, Eliya, Adar Maoz, and Zohar Or. Through the birth of each one of them, I learned more about freeing, relaxing, and empowering my vulva and bringing life into the world! Thank you to my sister Prema Shakti and my brother Kobi for their loving hearts, understanding, and constant support! Thank you to my friends Naama, Karuna, Mor and Sharon who helped me put into words what was clear to me without words. Thank you to Vered and Nurit for the endless support. Thank you to Shirit who read parts of this book. Thank you to Keren Levana, Dasi Elad, Naama Teva, Michaela, and Avi Newman who added their life knowledge to the content of the book. Thank you to the late Shlomi who looked into my eyes with his deep blue eyes, thanked me for writing this book, asked that I publish it, and reminded me how important it is.

---

18. The name of the book in Hebrew, which means to relax, release, empower your vulva.

A special thanks to Amir for his partnership on this journey, and for awaking me to explore the essence of the feminine and the masculine, the forgiveness between the two, and the choice of partnership and creation from a place of respect and love for both of these qualities, which motivated me to write this book. Thanks to Noa, the editor of this book, for her cooperation in making this book what it is today. Thank you for your patience with my pace, for listening, and for your sensitivity and comments that enlightened the way. Thank you Smadar Miller, my heart sister, for holding my hand when I jumped into the unknown and for continuing to believe that the book will come to light in the moments when I lost faith. Thanks to Smadar Dvorah Levi for being in my life, and for the infinite cleanses and choice to shine so much light and love on my path. Thank you to many more people that were kind to me, giving me strength along the way, asking questions, and awakening inside me the spark to keep writing. Thank you to the Beit Keshet community in all its diversity, which is a home for me to go to and return to every day. Thank you to the community of women in my life.

Special Thanks to Yinon & Suri Simha for providing motivation and support in the making of the English edition.

Thank you, Gabi, for your great translation, for your amazing ability to feel the spirit of the book, and for translating the book with precision and clarity.

Thank you to Benny Carmi and the great team at eBookPro, which gave me great direction for the English edition.

Special thanks to Tamara Lemesh for reading, and for the accuracy and clarity you helped me bring to the English edition. Thank you Aviva Shlimovitz for reading the whole book in English. Thank you Keren Mordoch, Ronda Joy Eagle, Shira Kranot, Ronit Netter, and Amir Koren for reading parts of the English edition.

Thank you, Daphne Meiri-Friedman, for the help with the wording and accuracy of the words in English.

I am grateful for my courage to walk with determination and blessings, to discover, and to be more of who I am in the world! Thank you — I choose life!

Made in the USA
Las Vegas, NV
07 October 2024

96391531R00144